A Manager's Guide to Self-development

A Manager's Guide to Self-development

FIFTH EDITION

Mike Pedler, John Burgoyne, Tom Boydell

The **McGraw·Hill** Companies

London   Boston   Burr Ridge, IL   Dubuque, IA   Madison, WI   New York   St. Louis
San Francisco   Bangkok   Bogotá   Caracas   KualaLumpur   Lisbon   Madrid   Mexico
Milan   Montreal   New Delhi   Santiago   Seoul   Singapore   Sydney   Taipei   Toronto

1999

A Manager's Guide to Self-development
Fifth Edition
Mike Pedler, John Burgoyne, Tom Boydell

ISBN-10: 0077114701
ISBN-13: 978 0077114701

 **Professional**

Published by McGraw-Hill Professional
Shoppenhangers Road
Maidenhead
Berkshire
SL6 2QL
Telephone: 44 (0) 1628 502 500
Fax: 44 (0) 1628 770 224
Website: www.mcgraw-hill.co.uk

British Library Cataloguing in Publication Data
A catalogue record for this book is available from the British Library

Library of Congress Cataloguing in Publication Data
The Library of Congress data for this book is available from the Library of Congress

Typeset by Gray Publishing, Tunbridge Wells, Kent
Cover design by Jan Marshall
Printed and bound in the UK by Bell and Bain Ltd, Glasgow

McGraw-Hill books are available at special quantity discounts.
Please contact the Corporate Sales Executive

The **McGraw·Hill** Companies

Contents

Acknowledgements

Our thanks to the many people who have contributed to this book; who taught us and from whom we have borrowed. Especial thanks to Justine Pedler who, in 1985, toothcombed the first edition and took out the sexism, ethnocentricism and sundry other embarrassments.

Part 1

Introduction

The Philosophy of this Book

1

This book, which is an aid to management self-development rather than a repository of facts and theories, is based on a simple fundamental premise:

> *that any effective system for management development must increase the person's capacity and willingness to take control over, and responsibility for, events – particularly for themselves and their own learning.*

Whilst this is not a new concept, it is one that is not always recognized. The standard approach to training and development has been that of learning to get the right answer from authority figures – teachers, experts, bosses, parents – in other words, to do things 'properly'. In recent years, views have changed considerably. The emphasis has shifted from *training* to do things right, to *learning* to improve, to push out the frontiers of knowledge and performance – in other words, to do things better.

If asked to think about how we have learned, many of us may think first of what we have been taught. Yet less than 20% of significant learning comes in this way. Our research shows that if you ask people how they have learned the things that are really important to them, 80% comes from tackling the challenging situations in life.[1] Moreover, in solving these problems we don't just deal with the immediate difficulty; we become better at solving problems in general. To a large extent, problem solving is learning.

Dealing with live problems is the fundamental managerial process, and it can also be the source of your significant learning – as long as you know how to learn from your experiences. When it comes to a 'crunch' decision such as selecting for a key appointment, what really matters is track record – whether the person has dealt successfully with difficult situations before. Completing formal management development programmes does not usually carry a lot of weight in these circumstances.

The implications are clear: to learn and to progress, first recognize the key management and leadership challenges, get into the action, reflect upon and learn from your experiences – and be seen to have done so.

Changing organizations

This new Fifth Edition of *A Manager's Guide to Self-development* sees many changes from the first edition of almost 30 years ago. Whilst the title is as relevant as it was then, our ideas about what makes for good management and leadership in organizations have evolved and changed.

Leaders and managers today need to be more than ambitious in simple career terms. Success used to mean climbing higher and higher on the organizational climbing frame, with the occasional bold leap across to a higher level on an adjacent structure. But many of these climbing frames have collapsed in recent years: they have broken up, shrunk and become 'leaner' and 'flatter'. The grim experience for some managers has been of throwing each other off the frame to make room for the survivors, who get used to sideways moves and increased responsibilities. In this reality, just having a job becomes more prized, and sideways moves can offer variety and development opportunities.

There is now a realization that success and satisfaction do not necessarily come from 'possessing' a large chunk of managerial territory in an invulnerable blue chip company, but from being part of a well run and effective organization which knows what it is doing, where it is going and what part each person's unique contribution can make. This has been the significance of the 'Excellence' movement of the 1980s,[2] the Total Quality movement[3] and, more recently, the 'Learning Company' idea.[4] People want to work in organizations which they believe are good, which know why they are good and know how they can stay that way.

Working together to do better things

In good organizations, everyone becomes more self-managing, aligning themselves with others through working to shared values and missions, rather than being directed by the external regulation of job descriptions and hierarchical supervision. Information technology also speeds this trend, distributing knowledge widely to make self-management more possible. Yet, at the same time, this is also the era of performance management where, driven by central targets, managers become local leaders, getting people enthused about learning to do things better – to improve themselves and their performance.

The downside of these performance and modernization efforts stems from their focus on easily measurable targets. These all too often result in the short term and the urgent pushing out the important and the long term. Simple targets can result in unhelpful competitions between individuals, teams and departments and the 50% of us who are 'below average' get punished rather than rewarded for our efforts.[5]

Many people now see the world as too complex to manage in these ways. Simple solutions may create worse problems elsewhere, and solving problems often means listening to the many and diverse stakeholders who want their voices to be heard. This requires managers to see the wider picture and appreciate the views of others who are 'different from us'. Organizational challenges cannot be tackled in isolation, they demand collaborative working with other individuals, teams, departments and agencies. 'Joined-up action' is essential, not only to do things better but to do better things together.[6]

What is self-development?

It has yet to be shown that formal leadership and management development programmes have much impact on organizational performance. Why is this? One possibility is that they may, unintentionally, encourage people to be less self-reliant. These programmes teach leadership, finance, strategy and so on, but the message is in the medium. The messages from formal development programmes are:

> *There is an expert for every type of management problem; don't try to solve it on your own – call in the experts.*

> *You don't know how to learn? Don't worry; you don't need to. We're here to manage that for you. If you need a 're-tread', don't try to do it yourself, come back to us.*

Such messages deskill people. This book has a different message; in our view:

> *Self-development is personal development, with the person taking primary responsibility for their own learning and for choosing the means to achieve this. Ultimately, it is about increasing your capacity and willingness to take control over, and be responsible for, events.*

Self-development can mean many things:

- developing specific qualities and skills
- improving your performance in your existing job
- advancing your career … or
- achieving your full potential as a person.

This book is an invitation to work on these aspects of your own personal and professional development, and an opportunity to help with the development of other people around you and thereby make a wider contribution to doing better things. Good luck.

References

1. Boydell TH, Pedler MJ and Burgoyne JG. *Management Self-development*. Prague: Czech National Training Fund, 1999.
2. Peters TJ and Waterman RH. *In Search of Excellence*. New York: Harper & Row, 1982.
3. Deming WE. *Out of the Crisis*. Cambridge: Cambridge University Press, 1986.
4. Pedler MJ, Burgoyne JG and Boydell TH. *The Learning Company: A Strategy for Sustainable Development*. Second Edition. Maidenhead: McGraw-Hill, 1996.
5. Kohn A. *Punished by Rewards; The Trouble with Gold Stars, Incentive Plans, A's, Praise and Other Bribes*. Boston: Houghton Mifflin, 1993.
6. Boydell TH. *Doing Things Well, Doing Things Better, Doing Better Things*. Sheffield: Inter-Logics, 2003.

Part 2

Planning Your Self-development

Planning Your Career

3

This chapter defines what we mean by a career and how careers are made in leadership and management. We discuss the career 'pipelines' and patterns in large and small businesses and the levels of leadership and management capability needed in all successful organizations. The chapter closes with an activity to help you reflect on your career to date and to plan for your next steps. This career planning will help you make the best use of the rest of this book.

Introduction

How many hours have you spent thinking about and planning:

- your last holiday?
- finding the house or apartment that you live in?
- choosing the purchase of your last car or laptop, music player, camera, etc.?
- your life and career?

Now rank order these: first in terms of the amount of time you spent on each, and second in order of their importance.

Are you giving enough attention to your life and career planning?

As you are reading this book you are probably interested in your career, and in this chapter we look at career planning in the broad context of life as a whole. This can help with a wide range of issues, for example:

- You may be wondering whether or not you want to become a leader or manager?
- You may be wondering whether you could be a manager, either in terms of your abilities and talents, or in terms of creating opportunities for this kind of work?

- On the other hand, you may have been a leader or manager for some time, and are now faced with questions such as: What is my next step?
- Another possibility is that you have gradually taken on managerial work without any formal training or briefing, and are wondering is there is more you ought to know, or things you could do better.
- Or perhaps you are becoming aware that something is wrong with the way you are balancing (or not!) the demands of your work with your family needs?
- Or again perhaps you have a feeling that something is missing? OK, you're getting on reasonably well in your job, but so what? What do you *really* want from life? Are you going to achieve it the way things are going?
- Finally, perhaps you are faced with a crisis such as redundancy, illness or separation? How are you handling this? What does it mean, not only in terms of loss, but also by way of providing a turning point?

The ways in which people become managers or leaders are many and various. This is partly because of the complexity of career patterns, which seem to get more complicated every year.

Career or job?

A career can be seen as a journey; are you now in the middle of this, nearer the beginning or perhaps towards the end? As in any journey, where you have come from and where you are now affects where you can go next. Yet, the past does not determine the future. Do you want to carry on in the same direction and in the same kind of career? Or is it time to go in a different direction?

When we talk about career, we don't necessarily mean those apparently smooth journeys offered in banking, insurance or the civil service (these 'careers for life' are less smooth and less common than they were). When we say career, we mean *the pattern or biography of your working life*. This includes the list of jobs on your CV and especially the story you tell people about what you have done so far, and what you intend to do from now on.

At this point, you may be thinking: 'I haven't got a career, it's just a job'. OK, but in the sense of the biography of a working life, everyone has a career, even where this involves doing the same job, as a doctor, as a plumber or as a gardener. There is always still plenty to learn in most jobs, especially about organizing, managing and leading the work.

Of course, your career is only part of the story of your life. Planning your career is part of this larger project, and it includes managing your work/life balance. The place of work in our lives changes over time, but work habits, such as travelling a lot or working long hours, can persist even when they no longer fit. What do you want from work NOW – money, esteem, networks, friends, power, to contribute more to society? Motivations in work change at different points in our lives.

Developing leadership and management ability

In occupations such as law, medicine, teaching, aviation or electrical contracting, professional learning is mainly carried out before starting the work. This is not the case in leadership and management, which is mainly learned on the job. About 12% of higher education students are studying management or business studies, but not all of them go on to this work, and employers do not necessary prefer them, either to other graduates or to people coming in by other routes.

Most leaders and managers have no formal qualification for doing this work. One argument is that these are general life skills acquired in the 'university of life' so that anyone who can run a household – dealing with people, money, material resources and so on – can also run a business. In any case, much of how we learn to lead and manage is learned informally as we go along in our careers. However, this does not mean that it can't be done better.

Leading, managing and careers

Leading and managing come into people's careers in different ways. For example:

Most people do not set out to be career managers or leaders. Research suggests that about two-thirds of managers are doing this as a second (or third or fourth) career. Look at the backgrounds of senior people and they have usually spent their early years in a technical or professional function. They have 'shaded into' leadership from being accountants, buyers, scientists, receptionists, IT specialists and so on. For example, a designer starts on technical design, then becomes involved in a design team, and finds themself doing the costings, or organizing the project timetable or presenting the design and arguing for its adoption; in other words, taking on many of the things associated with leadership and management. This makes sense because, in many settings, people need to be seen to know enough about what they are doing in order to be managers or leaders.

The other third of people have been career leaders and managers from the start, perhaps by joining a general management training scheme in a large organization, or by starting low on the ladder of supervision and moving up. A managerial career can embrace many jobs, from organizing a small project or group of people to being the senior person in a large business or public sector enterprise. Many of the processes of organizing people, resources, information and money stay the same, but the scale and nature of the challenges vary enormously.

A third important point is that about 50% of managers and leaders work in small organizations or SMEs. These include all types of small businesses from building firms to care homes in the private, public or not-for-profit sectors. Running small concerns can be very different from managing in large organizations, yet careers can often move between large and small, for example, when small enterprises are taken over by bigger ones or where people leave larger organizations to become 'their own bosses'. The outsourcing trend sometimes means that people from large businesses find themselves doing the same work in a smaller concern and perhaps selling the service back to their previous employer.

Career pipelines in large organizations

There are many kinds of leadership and managerial work in big organizations, and many ways to progress your career. All large concerns are hierarchical to some degree, and careers tend to be about rising to the appropriate level whilst performing effectively on the way.

Many big companies and agencies put great effort into managing the careers of their leadership and managerial cadres. One popular model, The 'Leadership Pipeline',[1] has a spectrum of seven levels of managing from managing yourself to running a global enterprise (see below). Moving from one level to the next requires the development of new abilities and marks a key transition. From an organizational point of view, the trick is to have the right numbers of people at the right points in the pipeline to ensure good quality succession, now and in the future. Organizations are therefore prepared to put particular efforts into helping people through these transitions rather than just to relying on the natural processes of learning from experience.

Do these seven types of management in Fig. 3.1 make sense to you? If so, where is your career at now? Are you currently working on any of the transitions?

The model suggests that we all start by *managing ourselves* and our work, perhaps moving on to *managing others* in small teams, and then to *managing managers*, or groups of teams through their managers. As operational teams tend to work in functions like production or finance, the *functional manager* has to understand the function in order to manage both it and its contribution to the business as a whole. Beyond this is the *business manager*, who is part of the general management team coordinating a business unit, and in very large organizations business units may be organized into groups, e.g. in oil companies where 'upstream' groups handle the exploration and extraction of oil, 'midstream' groups managing shipping and refining and 'downstream' groups focus on marketing and distribution. Each group may have several large business units that need coordinating by *group managers*. Finally, *enterprise management* is the strategic direction of the whole concern.

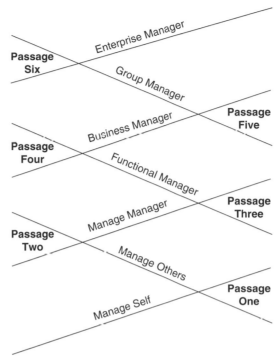

Note: Each passage represents a major change in job requirements that translates to new skill requirements, new time horizons and applications and new work values. Based on work done initially by Walter Mahler and called Critical Career Passages.

Figure 3.1 Critical career passages in large organizations. From Charan, R., Drotter, S. and Noel, J. The Leadership Pipeline: How to Build the Leadership Powered Company. *San Francisco: Jossey Bass, 2001. Reproduced with kind permission*

This model does not fit all organizations, or all career journeys, but it might help you to think about the different kinds of leadership and management in your organization and the passages and transitions involved. Is there a transition that you need to prepare for now?

Careers and small businesses

The Leadership Pipeline does not work for small organizations. In a small business these activities, from managing self to enterprise management, all run together. This can make small business management a more interesting challenge. 'Work on the business not in the business' is a reminder to owner-managers not to be too deeply involved with the day-to-day work of the enterprise. This is a transition that all successful leaders of small organizations need to learn their way through.

The small business leader should learn and grow with the business: through the pioneer stages of setting up and getting started, through the more analytical stages of introducing management systems to regularize what gets done and then on to the change management and development of the established concern.

Another distinction about working in small business and enterprise (including public and not-for-profit sector social enterprise) is between working *for* the business, working *in* the business and working *on* the business.

You can think of these as the work of workers, managers and leaders:

- Working *for* the business means doing the primary work through which it earns its livings for fulfils its task(s).
- Working *in* the business means doing all the arranging and managing that needs to be done to get the primary work done and delivered.
- Working *on* the business means standing back from the business and working out how it can be improved and developed.

Levels of leadership and management capability

All managers and leaders can use Jim Collins' (2001)[2] levels of management and leadership capability (Fig. 3.2). Collins suggests that these qualities sustain performance over time and move businesses from just being 'good' to being 'great'. In his model, each succeeding level of ability builds on the one(s) below and can be applied to any organizational setting, large or small, public or private.

These levels have some similarities with the career stages of the Leadership Pipeline:

- Level 1 suggests the capable individual who does a good job and manages themselves, but is not responsible for anyone else.
- Level 2 people make a good contribution to teamwork, in addition to their particular task performance.
- Level 3 people exercise more direct responsibility for organizing other people and resources to get things done, either in the team on a larger scale.
- Level 4 is seen as leadership and involves galvanizing peoples' commitment and energy in pursuit of a shared goal.
- Level 5 leadership denotes the intense professional will coupled with deep personal humility that Collins sees as the key to building the organizational cultures that sustain success over long period of time.

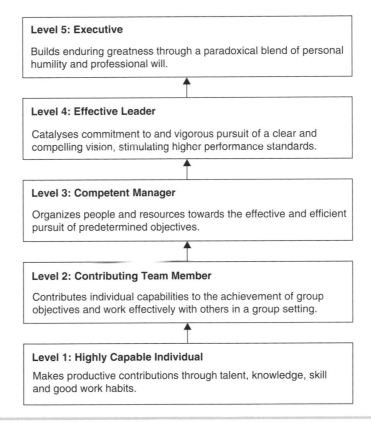

Figure 3.2 *Collins' levels of leadership. Adapted from Collins, J.* Good to Great. *London: Random House, 2001. Adapted with kind permission*

A Career Planning Activity

Here is a Career Planning Activity that combines these ideas of leadership and managerial careers, which will help you to:

- locate where you are now
- plot how you have got there
- note the transitions in your career so far
- consider how you made them
- project where you would like to go from here
- note the transitions that may be required now and in the future
- think about how you will make them.

Manager of:	
Enterprise	
Group	
Business	
Function	
Manager	
Others	
Self	
Roles ↑ **Capabilities** →	Individual team manager leader executive

Figure 3.3   A Career Planning Activity – large organizations

Follow these steps and plot them on either Fig. 3.3 or Fig. 3.4.

1. Locate where you are now:
    Consider where you are now on the grid in Figs. 3.3 or 3.4 (or both) – which point best describes where you are now?

2. Now plot how you have got there:
    Think back through your career history and assess your progress. In terms of the grid, have you progressed mainly through the responsibilities you have taken on – the vertical dimension – or though the growth of your own capabilities – the horizontal dimension?

3. Note the transitions you have made:
    Can you identify any key transitions in your career – like those implied in the Leadership Pipeline? (transitions are step changes where something quite new is required).

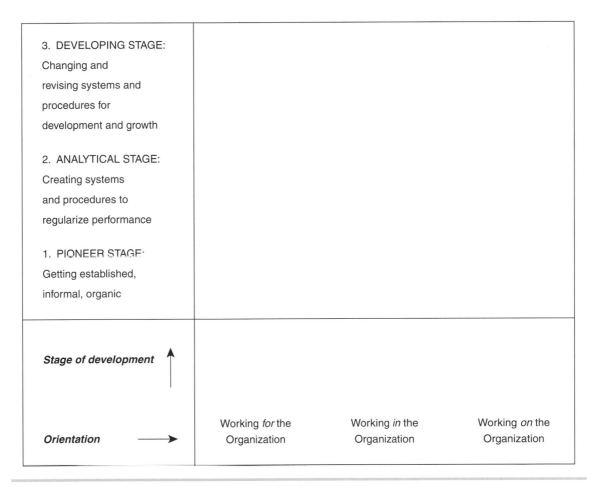

Figure 3.4 A Career Planning Activity – small organizations

4. Now consider how you made these transitions:
   How did you manage or cope with these transitions? Did you have any formal help, e.g. courses or programmes? Did you have any informal help such as coaching, mentoring? Or did you work it out for yourself? And, if so, how?

5. Now, project where you would like to go from here:
   Looking at the grid and where you have put yourself, where might you go next (this includes staying where you are, or going back to an earlier stage)? Now ask yourself: Is this what I want? Why do I want it? Is what I want feasible?

6. Note the transitions that may be required now and in the future and

7. Think about how you will make them:
   Consider what kinds of transitions you will need to make in the future, and also whether you are in one now. What are the nature of these transitions, in terms of both the role or work you do (vertical dimension) and what you bring to them in terms of your own abilities (horizontal dimension).

As with all the activities in this book, this Career Planning Activity is designed to be tackled alone; however, career planning will particularly repay the effort of discussing it with a trusted friend or colleague, including any training or development advisers that you may know.

References

1. Charan R, Drotter S and Noel J. *The Leadership Pipeline: How to Build the Leadership Powered Company.* San Francisco: Jossey Bass, 2001.
2. Collins J. *Good to Great.* London: Random House, 2001.

4

The Qualities of Successful Managers and Leaders

This book is a programme for self-development based on the qualities of the effective manager or leader. Before going on to outline these qualities, and explain why we think they contribute to successful managing, pause here and jot down your own views. What do you think:

- leadership and management *is*? What are the main features of this job?
- are the main qualities required to be a successful manager and leader?

Our framework of *The 11 Qualities of the Effective Manager* is based on a research project and also from our own experience of managerial and leadership work. The research project identified the qualities that were found more often in successful managers than in those judged to be less successful. Successful managers were those who had risen to senior posts or who were significantly younger on average for their level of seniority ('fast trackers') or, most importantly, managers of any age or level who were seen as doing their jobs with above average effectiveness.[1]

The research identified 10 attributes which were more often possessed by the successful managers, to which we have added another. These *11 Qualities of the Effective Manager* form the basis for the self-development programme provided in this book:

1. command of basic facts
2. relevant professional knowledge
3. continuing sensitivity to events
4. analytical, problem-solving and decision/judgement-making skills
5. social skills and abilities
6. emotional resilience
7. proactivity – inclination to respond purposefully to events
8. creativity
9. mental agility
10. balanced learning habits and skills
11. self-knowledge.

The 11 Qualities of the Effective Manager fall into three groups, which are also three different levels. Qualities 1 and 2 are the foundation level: they represent two kinds of basic knowledge and information that any leader or manager needs in making decisions and taking action.

The second level of Qualities 3–7 consists of the specific skills and attributes that directly affect behaviour and performance. Quality 3 – *Continuing Sensitivity to Events* – is the means by which people acquire the basic knowledge and information involved at the foundation level of Qualities 1 and 2.

Qualities 8–11 form the third or 'meta' level. These are the abilities that enable people to develop and deploy the second-level skills and capacities of Qualities 3–7. They are called 'meta-qualities' because they help people to develop the situation-specific skills needed in particular contexts (see Fig. 4.1).

Many of these 11 Qualities are interconnected – that is, possession of one contributes to possession of another. Here is a short explanation of each of them.

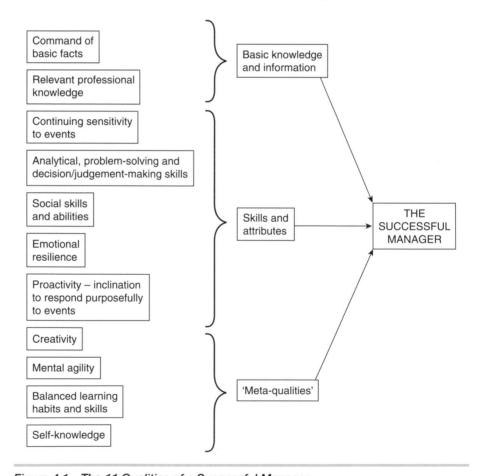

Figure 4.1   The 11 Qualities of a Successful Manager

Basic knowledge and information

1. *Command of basic facts.*
   Successful managers and leaders know what's what in their organizations. They have a command of such basic facts as goals and plans (long- and short-term), product knowledge, the roles and who's who in the organization, the relationships between various units, their own job and what's expected of them. If they don't store all this information, they know where to get it when they need it.

2. *Relevant professional knowledge.*
   This includes all 'technical' and specialist knowledge, e.g. information technology, marketing techniques, engineering knowledge, relevant legislative, financial or human resourcing expertise and also the essential background knowledge of management and leadership principles and theories, e.g. planning, organizing, motivating, team-building, performance managing and so on.

Skills and attributes

3. *Continuing sensitivity to events.*
   People vary in the degree to which they can sense what is happening in a particular situation. The successful manager is relatively sensitive to events and can tune in to what's going on. Leaders need to be perceptive and open to information – 'hard' information, such as facts and figures, and 'soft' information, such as the feelings of other people. People with this sensitivity are able to respond in appropriate ways to situations as they arise.

4. *Analytical, problem-solving and decision/judgement-making skills.*
   Managers and leaders are very much concerned with making decisions. Decisions can sometimes be made logically, using appropriate techniques, but they often require the ability to weigh the pros and cons in uncertain or ambiguous situations. This calls for a high level of judgement and even intuition. Managers and leaders must therefore develop judgement skills, including the ability to cope with ambiguity and uncertainty; and learn to strike a balance between objective logic and the necessity at times to be guided by subjective feelings.

5. *Social skills and abilities.*
   One old definition of managing is 'getting things done through other people', and although this is inadequate today, it does point to the key attribute of interpersonal skills. Any successful leader or manager develops a range of interpersonal and social skills: communicating, coaching, negotiating,

persuading, selling, networking, resolving conflicts and working with authority and power.

6. *Emotional resilience.*

All responsible jobs involve emotional stress and strain. This is a natural consequence of working in demanding situations, meeting targets and deadlines, dealing with dilemmas, decisions and conflicts, within a context of uncertainty and ambiguity.

Successful people have to resilient to cope. 'Resilient' means not only that we are able to keep going but also that when feeling stressed we don't get thick-skinned and insensitive, and cope by maintaining self-control and by 'giving' or bending to some extent.

7. *Proactivity – an inclination to respond purposefully to events.*

Effective leaders and managers work towards a purpose or goal, and do not merely respond to demands. At times, everyone has to respond to the needs of the instant situation, but in making their response the successful manager considers also the longer term, whereas the less successful responds to the immediate pressure in a relatively unthinking or uncritical way. Proactivity also includes seeing the job through, being dedicated and committed, having a sense of mission and taking responsibility for things that happen rather than passing the buck to someone else.

Meta qualities

8. *Creativity.*

By creativity we mean the ability to come up with unique responses to situations and to have the insight to recognize and adopt useful new approaches. Creativity is not just about having new ideas oneself, but also having the ability to recognize and encourage good ideas coming from other people.

9. *Mental agility.*

Although related to general intelligence, the concept of mental agility includes the ability to grasp problems quickly, to think of several things at once, to switch rapidly from one problem or situation to another, to see quickly the whole situation (rather than ponderously ploughing through all its components), and to 'think on one's feet'. Given the hectic and ever-changing nature of organizational life, mental agility is an essential quality for success.

10. *Balanced learning habits and skills.*

The importance of learning skills is one of the more recent discoveries of research on managerial and leadership work. Data from observing and interviewing managers show that a significant proportion of their success can be explained by the presence or absence of habits and skills related to learning:

- Good learners *use a range of different learning processes* from receiving formal and informal inputs from training courses or coaching, to reflection – the personal process of analysing and reorganizing their experiences and ideas – which can lead to discovery learning, or the generating of personal meaning from one's own experiences.
- Successful people *are more independent as learners*; they take responsibility for the 'rightness' of what is learned, rather than depending passively and uncritically on authority figures such as teachers or other experts to define 'the truth'.
- Successful managers *are capable of abstract as well as practical thinking*; they can relate and connect concrete ideas to abstract ones (and vice versa). This ability, sometimes known as a 'helicopter mind', enables people to generate their own theories from practice, and to develop their own practical ideas from theory.
- Effective managers and leaders are more likely to have *a wider view of the nature of the skills involved* in their work. For example, they are more likely to recognize the range of abilities as presented in this model of *The 11 Qualities of the Effective Manager*, than to see their work as a unitary activity, involving, for example, simply dealing with staff or making decisions.

11. *Self-knowledge.*

Whatever each of us does is affected not only by the way we see our job or role, by also by our goals, values, feelings, strengths, weaknesses, and a host of other personal factors. To maintain their self-command, any successful leader or manager must be aware of these self-attributes and the part they play in influencing their actions. The successful manager therefore needs the skills of introspection.

Qualities or competencies?

In recent years, the idea of competencies has become very popular in the training and development world, and considerable efforts go into identifying competencies for a range of jobs, including those of managers and leaders.

We prefer the word 'qualities' for the reasons listed below, but, whatever the term used, although it is useful to have frameworks to give people an idea of the kinds of knowledge, skills, abilities and so on that may be appropriate in a given job, it is misleading to use any such framework rigidly. The person doing the job should be the final judge of what is useful in performing it effectively.

We offer *The 11 Qualities of the Effective Manager* as a guide – not as a right answer – take it or leave it, take some of it, modify it, add to it, it's up to you.

No-one is against competence, a wholly admirable thing to give or to receive. The dangers appear, especially in the sort of discretionary work that most leaders and managers do, when *single, external measures* are used to define competence and, by implication, incompetence. We hold that all skills and abilities are *personal qualities*, learned, exercised and owned by individual people. The provider and the receiver of a service may define competence, incompetence or excellence in a way that does not make sense outside that context.

Finally, although we are keen to help people become more competent, we are also interested in performance that goes well beyond the meaning of this word. For people whose standards of work are well beyond the norm, the word 'competent' is faint praise. Such people – and they are found in every field – are creative artists in what they do, their work a personal expression of inner aspiration and outer expectation.

Summary: so what?

Everything written in this book is our opinion. To use it as an aid to your self-development, you must decide how much you share these views, and what they mean, personally, to you.

Having read this chapter, why not write down your reactions to it. How do you feel about it? Interested? Bored? Sceptical? Enthusiastic?

Activity 8 (in Part 3) involves keeping a personal journal to keep a note of your experiences in order to learn from them. If reading these first chapters has been a useful experience so far, you will enhance and consolidate your learning by working through Activity 8 now, before proceeding further.

Reference

1. Burgoyne JG and Stuart R. The nature, use and acquisition of managerial skills and other attributes, *Personal Review* 1976, **5**(4), 19–29.

5

Assessing Yourself and Setting Some Goals for Self-development

In Chapter 4 we introduced *The 11 Qualities of the Effective Manager*. This model provides the basis and structure for the activities that form the third part of this book.

One way of approaching the activities is to work through them in their order of appearance. In our view, a better way is to determine your own priorities and focus on these. This chapter gives you a way to do this, in three stages:

- diagnosing your priorities
- setting goals for self-development
- evaluating your progress.

Step 1. Diagnosis

The questionnaire below is based on *The 11 Qualities of the Effective Manager*. There are seven statements for each of the Qualities. Consider each statement in turn and decide whether it is:

- NOT true
- PARTLY true
  or
- VERY true

for you in your job and in your organization at this time.

At the end of each set of seven statements there is a box for you to total your score for the Quality being considered.

A second summary box invites you to decide – whatever the total score – how important this Quality is for you at this time. Is it a HIGH (Score = 3), MEDIUM (Score = 2) or LOW (Score = 1) priority?

NB. *We strongly recommend that you complete the questionnaire in two stages: first, go straight through ticking boxes for all 77 statements; and second, then work back through the sections adding up the totals and thinking about your priorities.*

We suggest this for two reasons: box ticking and adding/weighing up are two different activities and the one may distract from or distort the other; second, your priorities should be considered in the context of *The 11 Qualities of the Effective Manager* as a whole.

An Alternative to the Questionnaire: Conversation with a Partner

Although this questionnaire, like the rest of this book, is designed for you to work through alone, it is often helpful to work with somebody else. An appropriate partner – a friend, a coach, even your boss – can give you support, help you to act on ideas and provide useful feedback. Any partner must be committed to the role. An ideal situation might be where you both want to work on your self-development, so that you can help each other.

If you want to work with a partner, you can enrol a suitable person and work through all the statements in the questionnaire below. Take each one in turn and discuss it with your partner. Do you need to get better at this? Do you want to develop this quality further? Think about these statements, get your partner's views, compare them with your own and, when you have worked right through, complete the scoring, priority rankings and goals as for the questionnaire below.

THE 11 QUALITIES OF THE EFFECTIVE MANAGER QUESTIONNAIRE

For each statement (A1, A2, etc.), tick the box that best describes you in your job or organization. This statement is …

- **NOT** true for me (Score 0)
- **PARTLY** true for me (Score 1)
- **VERY** true for me (Score 2)

For example, if, in response to statement A1, you think that you actually do know a lot about what's going on around you, you would tick Box 0 next to that statement, e.g.

A. Command of basic facts

1. I find I don't know enough about what's going on around me. `0 | 1 | 2`

2. I make plans or decisions only to find later that they don't work because of something that I should have known but didn't `0 | 1 | 2`

3. I find that I need more information about the organization but I don't know how to get it. `0 | 1 | 2`

4. I don't have a clear understanding of how my organization works. `0 | 1 | 2`

5. Many of my colleagues seem to know more about the organization than I do. `0 | 1 | 2`

6. I don't really know who the important people are in my organization. `0 | 1 | 2`

7. I would like to know more about my organization's policies and future plans. `0 | 1 | 2`

TOTAL for A. Command of basic facts
(Add together the values of all the ticked boxes)

PRIORITY RANKING for A. Command of basic facts
[HIGH (3), MEDIUM (2) OR LOW (1)]

B. Relevant professional knowledge

1. I find that I don't know enough about the technical aspects of my job. `0 | 1 | 2`

2. Many of the people working with or for me seem to know more about various aspects of the job than I do. `0 | 1 | 2`

3. I would like to be more up to date on the professional aspects of my job. `0 | 1 | 2`

4. It would help me in my job if I spent more time reading specialist journals.

| 0 | 1 | 2 |

5. I have difficulty in keeping up with new techniques and developments.

| 0 | 1 | 2 |

6. I would welcome the opportunity to learn more about the theoretical background to my job.

| 0 | 1 | 2 |

7. I find that I don't seem to know enough about external factors such as market changes, new legislation and the like.

| 0 | 1 | 2 |

TOTAL for B. Relevant professional knowledge
(Add together the values of all the ticked boxes)

PRIORITY RANKING for B. Relevant professional knowledge [HIGH (3), MEDIUM (2) OR LOW (1)]

C. Continuing sensitivity to events

1. I don't seem able to pick up quickly what's going on.

| 0 | 1 | 2 |

2. I'm not very good at knowing or recognizing what other people are thinking or feeling.

| 0 | 1 | 2 |

3. I find that when something happens I'm only aware of part of what's going on – I overlook other aspects of the situation or problem.

| 0 | 1 | 2 |

4. Other people seem to notice more than I do about what's happening around them.

| 0 | 1 | 2 |

5. I don't really feel tuned-in to what's happening in a situation.

| 0 | 1 | 2 |

6. I have difficulty in knowing what other people are up to

| 0 | 1 | 2 |

7. I find myself surprised at the way other people react to what's happening.

`0` `1` `2`

TOTAL for C. Continuing sensitivity to events
(Add together the values of all the ticked boxes)

PRIORITY RANKING for C. Continuing sensitivity to events [HIGH (3), MEDIUM (2) OR LOW (1)]

D. Analytical, problem-solving and decision/judgement-making skill

1. I tend to dither when faced with a decision.

`0` `1` `2`

2. I find it difficult to trust my own judgement.

`0` `1` `2`

3. I have difficulty in analysing a situation into its various aspects.

`0` `1` `2`

4. I get confused when faced with several alternative courses of action.

`0` `1` `2`

5. I tend to jump to instant conclusions – acting quickly without spending much time thinking.

`0` `1` `2`

6. I find it difficult to weigh up the pros and cons of a solution to a problem.

`0` `1` `2`

7. When trying to make a decision I usually find that I've either got too much or too little information

`0` `1` `2`

TOTAL for D. Analytical, problem-solving and decision/judgement-making skill (Add together the values of all the ticked boxes)

PRIORITY RANKING for D. Analytical, problem-solving and decision/judgement-making skill [HIGH (3), MEDIUM (2) OR LOW (1)]

E. Social skills and abilities

1. I find that other people don't listen to me properly. | 0 | 1 | 2 |

2. I avoid telling people what I really think about them. | 0 | 1 | 2 |

3. There are times when I just don't seem to be able to get other people to see my point of view. | 0 | 1 | 2 |

4. I find that I simply cannot understand why someone else feels the way he or she does. | 0 | 1 | 2 |

5. Anger and conflict tend to frighten or upset me. | 0 | 1 | 2 |

6. I don't really see it as part of my job to step in between two people who don't get on with each other, as long as they do their job satisfactorily. | 0 | 1 | 2 |

7. Many of the people in my organization can't be trusted to get on with their job without constant supervision. | 0 | 1 | 2 |

TOTAL for E. Social skills and abilities (Add together the values of all the ticked boxes)

PRIORITY RANKING for E. Social skills and abilities
[HIGH (3), MEDIUM (2) OR LOW (1)]

F. Emotional resilience

1. I don't get emotional in my job – I just stick to the facts. | 0 | 1 | 2 |

2. Generally, I don't discuss my feelings or worries with other people. | 0 | 1 | 2 |

3. I often have difficulty in sleeping at night. | 0 | 1 | 2 |

4. I get worried because there's no way of knowing in advance whether or not I have made the right decision.

0	1	2

5. I worry about problems over and over in my mind.

0	1	2

6. When I'm nervous or tired I get moody and irritable and snap at people.

0	1	2

7. Most days I wake up with a 'Monday-morning' feeling.

0	1	2

TOTAL for F. Emotional resilience (Add together the values of all the ticked boxes)

PRIORITY RANKING for F. Emotional resilience [HIGH (3), MEDIUM (2) OR LOW (1)]

G. Proactivity – an inclination to respond purposefully to events

1. I'm passive rather than active.

0	1	2

2. I prefer to follow someone else's plans or instructions rather than act on my own initiative.

0	1	2

3. I find it difficult to stick at it when things aren't going too well.

0	1	2

4. I tend to temper initiative with caution.

0	1	2

5. I find that after a while there's no point in keeping up a losing struggle.

0	1	2

6. If forced to choose between two descriptions of myself, I would say that I am steady and reliable rather than adventurous and risk-taking.

0	1	2

7.   I feel a need to have more 'get-up-and-go'.

| 0 | 1 | 2 |

TOTAL for G. Proactivity – an inclination to respond purposefully to events (Add together the values of all the ticked boxes)

PRIORITY RANKING for G. Proactivity – an inclination to respond purposefully to events [HIGH (3), MEDIUM (2) OR LOW (1)]

H. Creativity

1.   I find it difficult to come up with new ideas.

| 0 | 1 | 2 |

2.   I am better at implementing well-tried solutions rather than experimenting.

| 0 | 1 | 2 |

3.   Other people seem better than me at thinking of new ways of solving problems.

| 0 | 1 | 2 |

4.   I get mental blockages when trying to think of new ways of doing things.

| 0 | 1 | 2 |

5.   I don't think that people with other specialist interests can offer me much in my particular job.

| 0 | 1 | 2 |

6.   Compared with other people, my ideas seem to be stuck in a rut.

| 0 | 1 | 2 |

7.   I'm not an imaginative person.

| 0 | 1 | 2 |

TOTAL for H. Creativity (Add together the values of all the ticked boxes)

PRIORITY RANKING for H. Creativity [HIGH (3), MEDIUM (2) OR LOW (1)]

I. Mental agility

1. I have difficulty in thinking on my feet in tricky situations.

0	1	2

2. I prefer to work on one thing at a time rather than be dealing with several things at once.

0	1	2

3. To see the whole situation one must carefully consider all the parts.

0	1	2

4. Once I get stuck into a task I try to remain with it rather than switch to something else and then back again.

0	1	2

5. 'Slow and steady wins the race' is a pretty good motto.

0	1	2

6. The trouble with my job is that I'm never left alone to get on with it – there are too many interruptions.

0	1	2

7. I'm not what you'd call a quick thinker.

0	1	2

TOTAL for I. Mental agility (Add together the values of all the ticked boxes)

PRIORITY RANKING for I. Mental agility [HIGH (3), MEDIUM (2) OR LOW (1)]

J. Balanced learning habits and skills

1. Experience is the only valid teacher.

0	1	2

2. I'm not able to convert my own experiences into valid theories.

0	1	2

3. If I hear of a new theory I find it difficult to translate it into practical terms relevant to my job.

0	1	2

4. When I get an idea I like, if possible, to have it checked out by an expert.

0	1	2

5. I like to have teachers or trainers give me a lot of information and ideas.

0	1	2

6. I'm the sort of person who goes around saying 'no one can tell me how to do my job'.

0	1	2

7. I dislike abstract thoughts and theoretical ways of talking about management.

0	1	2

TOTAL for J. Balanced learning habits and skills
(Add together the values of all the ticked boxes)

PRIORITY RANKING for J. Balanced learning habits and skills [HIGH (3), MEDIUM (2) OR LOW (1)]

K. Self-knowledge

1. I find it difficult to ask other people what they really think of me.

0	1	2

2. I don't think we should let our values and feelings affect the way we behave at work.

0	1	2

3. I don't spend much time thinking about myself – my strengths and weaknesses.

0	1	2

4. It's a good job we can't read the thoughts of others.

0	1	2

5. I'm basically a logical person, and I don't let my feelings influence me.

0	1	2

6. There's just not enough time in my job to sit around talking about how we feel about each other.

0	1	2

7. It's dangerous to be introspective.

0	1	2

TOTAL for K. Self-knowledge (Add together the values of all the ticked boxes)

PRIORITY RANKING for K. Self-knowledge [HIGH (3), MEDIUM (2) OR LOW (1)]

Step 2. Goal setting

When you have worked through *The 11 Qualities of the Effective Manager Questionnaire* and completed the totals and priority rankings, transfer your results into Columns 2 and 3 of Table 5.1.

Table 5.1 The 11 Qualities of the Effective Manager: scores and priority rankings

The 11 Qualities of the Effective Manager	2. TOTAL SCORES Min = 0; Maximum = 14	3. PRIORITY RANKINGS High (3), Medium (2) or Low (1)	4. GOALS With dates and targets
A. *Command of basic facts*	4	2	
B. *Relevant professional knowledge*	8	3	
C. *Continuing sensitivity to events*	4	2	
D. *Analytical, problem-solving and decision/judgement-making skill*	6	3	
E. *Social skills and abilities*	2	2	
F. *Emotional resilience*	4	1	
G. *Proactivity – an inclination to respond purposefully to events*	2	1	
H. *Creativity*	9 3	1	
I. *Mental agility*	3	1	
J. *Balanced learning habits and skills*	4	1	
K. *Self-knowledge*	2	1	

Analysis

Total scores

First, look over your total scores. The higher your score for any given Quality, the more likely you are to have a self-development need in that area. If you scored between:

- 0 and 4   you seem well developed in this Quality at this time
- 5 and 9   this **may well be** a developmental need for you
- 10 and 14   this is a **definite** developmental need for you.

If you have any scores of between 10 and 14, these suggest obvious areas for development. Scores of between 5 and 9 also indicate a likely need for development depending upon your circumstance and priorities. Even if your score is 4 or less for a given Quality, indicating that you are well developed in this respect, you may still wish to develop further this strength in yourself.

A key point about these scores is that they reflect your current situation. This can change at any time; which is where the priority rankings come in.

Priority rankings

Now consider your priority rankings – which of *The 11 Qualities of the Effective Manager* matter most to you – now and in the future?

If you have one or two very high scores then these might be the obvious choices. If they are all about the same, then you might choose by selecting areas that particularly appeal to you or that seem especially prized in your work environment at this time.

In any case, we suggest that you choose one, two or three areas at most to concentrate on now. As you progress; you can come back to the others, and it is well said that those with multiple priorities really have no priorities at all.

Goals

When you have chosen your priority areas, give yourself a specific target for that area, for example:

'By [choose a realistic date] I will have carried out all [or 3 or 50%, or whatever] the activities in this book which are related to this goal area.'

If you really want to test yourself, and create an 'output measure' for your learning, you could write yourself a second goal, specifying a change in your behaviour in this area, which you could verify by enrolling a colleague, for example:

'By [choose a realistic date] I will be [describe the desired behaviour, e.g. speaking up more in meetings, or managing my stress levels better, or whatever] as

independently verified by [put in name of colleague or boss or coach or other trusted person].'

Write your goals into Column 4 of Table 5.1.

Step 3. Evaluation

Review your progress and set new goals as you reach your targets. Have you achieved your goals in this area? Do you want to move to another? Even if you have completed the activities for a given goal area once, you might wish to continue to do them, as many of them are designed to be incorporated into your everyday way of working.

It helps a great deal at this point to discuss your progress with another person. If you chose the 'Conversation with a partner' alternative to the Questionnaire as outlined at the start of this chapter, then this will be very straightforward. If you have so far worked on your own, find someone to talk to – a friend, a trainer or perhaps a more senior and trusted person – who will help you evaluate your progress and think about future goals.

Conclusion

This chapter provides a way for you to diagnose your own self-development needs and set some realistic goals.

In Part 3 of this book, you will find the activities to help you in achieving these goals. The next chapter, Chapter 6, is a guide to selecting activities for developing each of *The 11 Qualities of the Effective Manager* as well as giving general guidelines on the use of the activities.

How to Select and Use the Activities

Having chosen your priorities and set yourself some goals, this chapter helps you select and use appropriate self-development activities from Part 3 of this book.

Selecting the Activities

Table 6.1 shows *The 11 Qualities of the Effective Manager* across the top and the 53 activities for management self-development down the left-hand side. A bold cross in any column indicates that this activity is designed to bring about *major learning* in that particular quality. A light cross indicates a secondary rather than a primary application; although the activity is not primarily designed for that quality, there is likely to be some learning pay-off in this area.

Look down the columns of your priority qualities and choose those activities relevant to your self-development goals. What is the right order in which to tackle activities? This is down to you, but here are three possibilities:

1. One strategy is to start with the activities that help you to 'learn how to learn'. The 'meta-qualities' of self-knowledge, balanced learning habits, mental agility and creativity are key to leaders and managers because they promote good self-development habits. These will also help you get the most out of the activities designed for other of *The 11 Qualities of the Effective Manager*.
2. An obvious alternative is to start with your most urgent learning goals, and choose activities appropriate to your greatest area of need.
3. If neither of these appeal to you, you could just dive in and try one or two of the activities, and then make up your mind what to do next as you go along. This 'suck it and see' approach allows you to get a feel for the kind of activities that suit you best.

Table 6.1 The Qualities/Activities Matrix

Learning area activities	Situational facts	Professional knowledge	Sensitivity to events	Analytical skills	Social skills	Emotional resilience	Proactivity	Creativity	Mental agility	Balanced learning habits	Self-knowledge
1. Know your facts	×		×								
2. Networking	×				×		×				
3. Managing your time	×	×		×							
4. Keeping up to date		×								×	
5. Find a mentor		×					×			×	
6. Communication tools		×			×		×				
7. Facts and assumptions			×		×						×
8. Personal journal			×	×						×	×
9. Use your power			×		×		×				
10. Differences and discrimination	×	×	×								
11. Political awareness			×		×		×				
12. Credulous listening			×		×					×	
13. The saturated life						×					×
14. Decision making				×							
15. Role set analysis	×			×							
16. Planning change				×			×				
17. Catastrophic contingencies				×		×	×	×			×
18. Asserting yourself					×	×	×				×
19. Handling conflicts			×		×	×					
20. Getting the best out of groups			×	×	×		×				
21. What are you like?				×	×						×
22. Getting to know you					×						×
23. Getting to Yes			×		×	×					
24. Collaborative working					×	×		×			
25. Be a coach!		×			×					×	
26. Difficult situations						×					

(continued)

Table 6.1 (*continued*)

Learning area activities	Situational facts	Professional knowledge	Sensitivity to events	Analytical skills	Social skills	Emotional resilience	Proactivity	Creativity	Mental agility	Balanced learning habits	Self-knowledge
27. Are you stressed?						×					×
28. Treat yourself well						×					×
29. Relaxation						×					
30. Fitness						×					
31. Manage your feelings					×	×					×
32. Stability zones						×					
33. The virtual revolution			×	×	×	×					
34. Be your own personal trainer						×	×				×
35. Who's the boss?				×	×		×				
36. Practising change			×			×	×				
37. Action planning				×			×				
38. Imaging			×				×	×			
39. Managing upwards					×		×				
40. Beyond 'yes … but …'				×				×			×
41. Generating new ideas				×				×			
42. Approaches to creativity								×			
43. Attribute alternatives								×			
44. Your multiple intelligences								×	×		×
45. Coping with complexity							×		×		
46. Just a minute					×				×		
47. A helicopter mind								×	×	×	
48. Managing your dependency										×	
49. Learning to learn			×							×	×
50. Study skills		×								×	×
51. Your learning cycle			×							×	×
52. Conversations with yourself								×			×
53. Backwards review			×								×

Using the Activities

There are many paths to self-development. Opportunities commonly found in organizations include:

- mentoring
- coaching/counselling
- appraisal
- internal rotation, attachment and placement
- external attachments and placements
- reading
- joining special projects
- committee membership
- discussion groups, working parties, meetings of professional bodies and institutes
- learning from one's own job and experience
- special activities.

However, many work experiences do not lead to development or learning. Some, such as committee work or professional gatherings, may be too predictable and routine; others, such as appraisal sessions, may be used as control rather than development mechanisms. This need not be so. With effort on your part, most work experiences can become enriching and rewarding, and we recommend that you scan all of the self-development opportunities open to you and take advantage of some of them. This book will help you learn from all these possibilities.

However, the main purpose of this book is to provide you with a 'starter pack' of activities to use as part of your self-development programme. The following notes will help you to get the most out of them.

Commitment

The more you put in, the more you get out. Physical fitness exercises don't work if you only pretend to do them, or do them half-heartedly, and it's the same with the activities in this book. There is no point in cheating. Here are two ways to support your commitment:

Working with a partner. All the activities can be done on your own, but you might get more benefit by working with a partner – a colleague or a friend. It doesn't matter *who* the partner is but they must be someone you can trust to listen to you and give you honest feedback. If you decide to work with a partner, 'Getting to know you' (Activity 22) provides an opportunity to build a useful helping relationship.

Working with support groups. This involves, say, four or more people, agreeing to try out the activities in their own time. At regular intervals (once or twice a month) they then meet to share experiences and help each other via feedback and discussion. Human Resource, or development managers might help if you want to set up such a group in your own organization. Alternatively, you could set up your own support group by inviting some colleagues or friends to join you. 'Collaborative working' (Activity 24) will help you prepare for this.

Action and learning

Each activity is designed around a three-stage model of learning (Fig. 6.1).

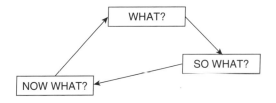

Figure 6.1   Doing the activities

What? This is the experience following the action. Each activity suggests some action for you to do, and then asks you to note your immediate observations of what happens. Writing down your observations and reactions is the first stage of learning from experience.

So what? Now think about what happened, and analyse your reactions and observations. What are your feelings? ideas? insights? and questions? This phase is important because it involves reflecting on your experiences and making sense of them.

Now what? This third phase is the most difficult. It involves taking stock of what you have done and what you have learned from it, and then deciding how this will change your behaviour. Now what? means making concrete plans for your future actions based on your learning. It is especially important to write these down, as they form the basis for evaluating your ongoing self-development.

Make the activities part of your normal life

Doing all the activities in Part 3 may not immediately make you the perfect manager or leader. However, we can guarantee that doing them will kick-start your self-development based on *The 11 Qualities of the Effective Manager* and encourage in you a learning process which will have a major impact over time.

Make these activity processes part of your normal working life and incorporate good learning habits into your everyday behaviour. You might do this by repeating certain activities that are particularly useful to you, perhaps with modifications to suit. With repetition you will notice the various skills and abilities growing as you do so. The 'Personal journal' (Activity 8) can be used to keep track of your progress in this way.

By repeating activities, modifying them, generating your own and gradually using all aspects of your everyday experiences as opportunities for experimentation, learning and self-development, you will become what someone once called a 'learning manager', and this book will have achieved its purpose.

Part 3

Activities for Management Self-development

Know Your Facts

All work involves making decisions and putting them into practice. Facts are inputs to decisions. However good you are at decision making, your decisions and actions will be wrong if they are based on inaccurate information. We distinguish here between situational and professional facts. Situational facts are things like the price of materials, the size of an order book, a customer's delivery deadline. Professional facts are to do with specialist management area like information management or financial reporting requirements.

Professional facts are distinct from professional skills and procedures. They are the professional inputs to *managerial* rather than *professional* decisions. The manager of a plant with a sophisticated technology may have a technical background sufficient to make *managerial* decisions, to plan, for instance, the plant's output and staffing, taking account of the need for maintenance. If the plant breaks down technically, the manager may choose to get involved in the technical/professional search for a solution, but this is temporary return to a technical/professional role. Here we are concerned with professional facts as inputs to managerial decisions, rather than with professional skills in dealing with professional problems.

Situational and professional facts vary in their permanence, from highly variable – like the price of services and the stock level of finished goods – to relatively permanent ones like the date of annual audit or the preferences of regular customers.

Reviewing your command of situational and professional facts

Once you have identified what you need to know in developing your command of situational and professional facts, it is probably fairly easy to get this knowledge. The problem is that we usually don't know what we don't know, and it is the data in the blind spots that we really need.

Consider the situation shown in Fig. A1.1.

What you need to do is to convert Cs into As, Ds into Bs and Bs into As.

The exercise below will help you to clarify what you already have in 'A' and 'B', add to it from 'C', and help you explore 'D'.

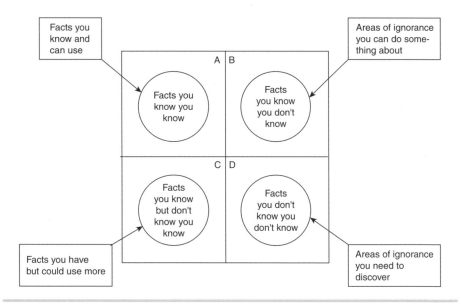

Figure A1.1   Four types of facts

Activity

Step 1

Imagine that someone important wants to check on whether you are really on the ball on the situational and professional facts concerning your job or role.

Take a piece of paper and write down as many key questions as you can think of about any facts of your job as it exists now. Imagine that you are compiling the test questions for *Mastermind*, with your job as the topic. Aim to get at least 10 or 12. Now write down all the answers to these questions.

Step 2

Now extend the list of questions and answers by any or all of the following:

(a) If you redesigned, developed, or extended your job in any way that you think desirable, what would this add to the list of questions and answers?

(b) What are the next possible moves in your career? What new facts would you need to have at your command to perform these future jobs?

(c) What kind of training and education are provided for people coming into your kind of work? What facts do they have that you haven't?

(d) Imagine showing your list to:
  (i)   your boss
  (ii) your staff
  (iii) your colleagues
  (iv) others in similar jobs to yourself
  (v)   anyone else with whom you are regularly in contact.

What do you think they might suggest that you add to the list?

(e) Show your list to some of the people mentioned in (d) and ask them. Exchange lists with someone in a similar job to yourself who has done this exercise and discuss them both.

NB. Point (e) is particularly important because of the 'don't-know-what-you-don't-know' factor; so second opinions greatly enhance the benefit you can get from this activity.

Follow-up

You probably know the answers to most of the new questions you have posed, but make a list of things you need to know about the others.

If any of them strike you as difficult, then other activities in this book related to the learning areas 'Sensitivity to events' and 'Balanced learning habits' (Table 6.1) will help.

Activity 2

Networking

Learning areas	**Situational facts:** Social skills: Proactivity

The effective manager knows not only 'what's what', but also 'who's who'. 'The Old Boys' Network' has often attracted anger partly because it has proved so effective for 'old boys' wanting to get on. Even more so today, networking has become an essential task and skill for all managers because so much depends upon good relationships and upon knowing where to connect with the distributed knowledge on any issue. To be effective we need a lot of contacts; we need to know what others do, how they can help us and how we can help them.

Activity

Step 1

The first step is to decide whom you are going to get to know. To start with, choose one person to get to know better and find out what they do. There are a number of ways of doing this, for example:

1. Look at an organization chart and choose someone in an area about which you know very little.
2. Use an internal telephone directory to the same end.
3. Pick a person from the offices or workplaces around you.
4. Choose someone whom you have seen about the place, without knowing who they are, or what they do.
5. Choose a person at random, the third person who enters a lift or walks into the canteen, or stick a pin into the internal telephone book.

Step 2

Having chosen your first potential contact, now get to know him or her.

This will be more difficult than it sounds, but less difficult than you imagine. You can explain frankly that you are trying to get to know more people or, if you prefer a more covert approach, just try to engage the chosen person in informal conversation.

Your goal should be to find answers to the following questions:

(a) What is the person's name?
(b) What is his or her job title?
(c) What does that job involve?
(d) How does this person see the main purpose of the job and its contribution to the organization? (Do you agree? If not, can you explore this difference?)
(e) What are his or her major goals, concerns, issues, problems?
(f) In what way can the person be of help to you?
(g) In what way can you be of help to him or her?
(h) Are there any ways in which the person's goals, needs or interests conflict with yours? If so, what can be done to lessen or overcome this conflict?

You will need to develop certain skills to get the person talking about these things. Some hints on how to do this are given in Table A2.1.

Table A2.1   Hints on getting another person to talk freely

---

1. If you want fairly long, descriptive answers, ask open-ended questions, such as:
   'What . . .?'
   'How do you . . .?'
   'Could you explain . . .?'
   'Can you give an example of . . .?'
   'How do you feel about . . .?'
   'Why do you . . .?'
2. Unless you want very specific, precise, short answers, avoid closed questions, such as:
   'Do you . . .?'
   'How often . . .?'
   'Is it true that . . .?'
   'How many . . .?'
3. Notice non-verbal cues, such as tone of voice, changes in posture, facial expression, eye movement, gestures, speech hesitancies.
4. Respond to non-verbal cues by using them to suggest further questions, by remarking on them, or by changing the subject, whichever you think most appropriate.
5. Check out and clarify what you are hearing (i.e. repeat in your own words what you think the other person has said, what is meant and how he or she feels).
6. If the other person talks mostly about feelings, it might be useful to ask about ideas or facts; on the other hand, if facts are offered at the time, then try asking about feelings.
7. From time to time, find out the other person's feelings about you and the process of the discussion.
8. All the time, ask yourself if you are prepared to be as open with the other person as you are asking him or her to be with you.

Step 3

Once you have made your first contact, repeat the activity, perhaps meeting at least one new person a week until you feel you have built your network to a good level.

Follow-up

Using this approach, you gradually build an excellent network of contacts throughout the organization and beyond. This network will help you stay tuned in to what's going on and provide you with information, help and support when needed. In turn, you will be helping others when they need you.

Networking is one of the arts of managing. This has always been the case but is now even more vital in the 'age of information', where success so often depends on making contacts not only within your own immediate sphere of influence but across many boundaries – for example, with colleagues in other departments, customers, suppliers, informal contacts in other organizations.

Gael and Stuart Lindenfield's *Confident Networking for Career Success and Satisfaction* (Piatkus, 2005) is easy to read, as is John Timperley's *Network Your Way to Success: Discover the Secrets of the World's Top Connectors* (Piatkus, 2002). Finally, our own book on leadership also contains two chapters on networks and networking: Pedler, Burgoyne and Boydell, *A Manager's Guide to Leadership* (McGraw-Hill, 2004).

There is lots of material on the web about networking – but 95% of it is about various aspects of IT. On the other hand, www.quintcareers.com/networking.html gives a number of other sites that are to do with networking for career management, albeit with a work flavour.

www.networking-coach.com is a Dutch networking consultant's site – with a version available in English. Much of it is about courses in The Netherlands, but there is an e-learning course delivered by e-mail which, at the time of writing, is free. This is well worth a try if you are interested.

Activity **3**

Managing Your Time

Time is a major scarcity for 21st century people. The opportunities for time spending become more numerous every year. We consume more and more and although we have time-saving devices, they also demand time for maintenance. We have to budget time as we budget money. We calculate the opportunity cost of spending time even with friends, relatives and loved ones.

Make a quick inventory of your free time for the rest of the week:

Hours

Monday

Tuesday

Wednesday

Thursday

Friday

Saturday

Sunday

Note down for each day how much free time you have. What is left after sleeping, eating, working and travelling? Then try putting down things you could do in this time, under three headings:

1.   Things I MUST do this week.

_____

_____

_____

_____

2.   Things I SHOULD do this week.

_____

_____

_____

_____

3.   Things I would LIKE to do this week (if only I had the time).

_____

_____

_____

_____

As this is a private list and for your eyes only, you can afford to be honest with yourself.
For example, have you included time for being with close friends and family? Time for doing nothing much? Time to recover from doing too much? Time for passing the time of day with all those other faces and acquaintances in your life?

A main purpose of the activity below is to gain some feeling of control over how your time is spent. This might involve cutting out unrewarding activities but it might also include looking for chunks of time in which to do things which you're not doing at the moment but which you ought or would like to be doing.

For example, a manager in a large retail company looked at the way she used working time. She discovered that she spent *three hours every day* overseeing and checking the work of her staff (and another hour each day taking lunch). On top of her own busy job, she had staff members who didn't accept responsibility and who did not exercise initiative. She had a weight problem, because she never had enough time to take exercise. What she could not see was that the way she spent time was linked to her other problems. How could members of staff exercise responsibility if she gave them no discretion – if their work was continuously checked? She could have gained another half hour by having a light lunch and a walk instead of her usual one-hour three-courser in the management dining room.

So, managing your time properly may increase others' effectiveness and capacity in addition to your own. It is also one of the keys to the thorny problem of delegation – are you spending your time on the right activities? We can see you're busy – but doing what?

Activity

Managing time is one aspect of leading yourself. One of the characteristics of the effective manager and leader is *proactivity* – being a self-starter, taking personal responsibility and getting something done. You can start here – in three steps:

1. *Recording* how your time is spent. (Before you can manage your time, you need to find out what you're doing with it.)
2. *Analysing* on what you spend your time.
3. *Making decisions* about the most effective use of your discretionary time.

Step 1

Record your activities at work for the next five days. You can design your own recording sheet or use the one given in Table A3.1.

Spend five days, *at least*, on this – the full value of the exercise cannot be gained from less.

Step 2

When you have at least five days' worth of data, now analyse your data sheets under four headings:

(a) *outcome*
(b) *type of work*
(c) *where does the work come from?*
(d) *delegation.*

Table A3.1   Recording sheet

TIME LOG

Day:_____ Date:_____

Describe WHAT HAPPENS in detail – the subject of meetings, phone calls, letters, reading, conversations. Note the DURATION of each happening. Note the NAME and POSITION of OTHER PEOPLE INVOLVED. Include even casual encounters.

Time	What happened?	Duration	People involved	Comments
9.00 9.30				
9.30 10.00				
10.00 10.30				
10.30 11.00				
11.00 11.30				
11.30 12.00				
12.00 12.30				
12.30 1.00				
1.00 1.30				
1.30 2.00				
2.00 2.30				
2.30 3.00				
3.00 3.30				
3.30 4.00				
4.00 4.30				
4.30 5.00				
5.00 5.30				

(a) OUTCOME

■ How successful were the various activities?

_____

_____

_____

■ Have you any habitual failures?

_____

_____

_____

(b) TYPE OF WORK

Divide your work tasks into three categories:

■ MUST do? (most important duties)

_____

_____

_____

■ SHOULD do? (next most important duties)

_____

_____

_____

■ Would LIKE to do? (least important duties)

_____

_____

_____

Allocate a theoretical percentage of your effort to each of these, e.g. 75%, 20% or 5%?

How much of your time are you spending on each set of activities compared to the 'correct' theoretical mix?

NB. *We often concentrate on things we are able to do or like doing at the expense of things which we find difficult. These difficult tasks may be the most vital ones.*

Another way of looking at this is to ask yourself what proportion of my time goes on:

■ *Leadership and managerial work* – planning, motivating, team building, etc.?

_____

_____

_____

■ *Professional skills* – exercising your old specialist professional skills?

_____

_____

_____

A common trap is the carrying over of professional work into the manager's job. You may need to exercise these skills part of the time, but exactly how much is appropriate:

10%?
15%?
20%?

And how much are you *actually* doing?

The *leadership and managerial* work may be the most difficult and you may be avoiding it – preferring the comfort of working in your old craft or field.

(c) WHERE DOES THE WORK COME FROM? From the …

■ Boss – is he or she delegating enough? Are they using you as a personal assistant?

_____

_____

_____

■ Staff – are they too dependent upon you?

_____

_____

_____

■ Self – are you setting yourself enough tasks?

_____

_____

_____

■ Elsewhere – where?

_____

_____

_____

How important are each of these?

(d) DELEGATION
For each task or event ask yourself:

■ Could this have been delegated?
■ If YES, to whom?

If NO, why not? (Your answer to this one should be really thoughtful.) Is it really your job or have you made yourself indispensable?

Step 3

After analysis it's time to make some decisions about how to spend your time.

(a) What things are you spending time on that you could either **cut out, cut down, or delegate**?

(b) What things are you not doing now that you should be – or what things should you **be doing more of**?

You can use your three job areas of MUST do; SHOULD do and Would LIKE to do for this.
   Make sure the MUST DOs are done!

(c) What actions will you **commit yourself to here and now**?

Action

1.   *Completed by:*

_____

_____

_____

2.   *Completed by:*

_____

_____

_____

3.   *Completed by:*

_____

_____

_____

4.   *Completed by:*

_____

_____

_____

etc.

Follow-up

Obviously you can repeat your time log any time you like to check out how you're functioning, when are your best times, and so on.

A few years ago there were numerous self-help books on time management. Currently these seem to be less in vogue, although typing 'time management' into a couple of well-known search engines produced 688,000,000 (yes 688 million) and 543,000,000 hits, respectively, so there's still quite an interest out there!

A good starter might be *The Time Management Pocketbook*, by Ian Fleming (Alresford: Management Pocketbooks, 5th edn, 2003). There are many little books in this series (www.pocketbook.co.uk) which provide succinct, readable summaries – perhaps a bit oversimplified but good value for money.

A relatively up-to-date book is Fergus O'Connell's *How to Do a Great Job... and Go Home on Time* (Financial Times Prentice Hall, 2005). This is not so much a '101 ways to make every minute count' book but takes a more thoughtful look at the nature of work-life balance and how to set about achieving it. If you do like the '101 ways' approach then you'll find about a fifth of that number in a book that follows the popular fashion of including an allegedly eye-catching phrase in its title, namely *Eat That Frog! 21 Great Ways to Stop Procrastinating and Get More Done in Less Time,* by Brian Tracy (Hodder and Stoughton, 2004). An altogether deeper and more thoughtful – indeed some would say spiritual – approach is described by Angus Jenkinson in his *From Stress to Serenity* (Sophia Books, 2003), whilst a proven favourite that has sold well over one million copies and is often reissued is *The Time Trap* – its current (2002) edition is by Alec MacKenzie and R. Alec MacKenzie, and is published by MJF Books.

When it comes to online resources, it's hard to choose from 688,000,000! If we discount those that refer to clocking-in machines and other approaches to what these days are referred to as 'time and attendance management systems', there's still a lot to choose from. Many colleges and universities – especially in the USA – post useful guides, most of which can readily be adapted to be of value to managers as well as to the students for whom they are primarily written. And there is a plethora of time management training courses to choose from.

If you are a dedicated user of Microsoft Outlook, you might like to try Sally McGhee's *Take Back Your Life Using Outlook* (Microsoft Press, 2004).

Keeping Up to Date

Learning areas	**Professional knowledge:** Balanced learning habits

Successful leaders and managers know what is going on. Good judgements rest on up-to-date professional knowledge. A good manager or leader needs to know not only about new developments in their specialist expertise but more generally about changes in markets, legislation, culture, fashions and so on.

The purpose of this activity is to encourage you to think about your personal strategy for keeping up to date and to suggest some ways of doing this.

Activity

Step 1

First, here are some questions to answer. Take your time and think about them before you answer.

(a) How much time do you spend READING in your field each week?

_____

_____

_____

(b) How much time do you spend LOOKING AT WEBSITES, USING ELECTRONIC CONFERENCES, NOTICE BOARDS, etc.?

_____

_____

_____

(c) How would you describe the way you read this material (e.g. scanning, gleaning, immersing yourself)?

_____

_____

_____

(d) Write down the names of the JOURNALS, NEWSLETTERS, WEBSITES, ELECTRONIC CONFERENCES, etc., that you use regularly in your field.

_____

_____

_____

(e) Which relevant JOURNALS, MAGAZINES, NEWSLETTERS, WEBSITES, etc., do you *not* see or read?

_____

_____

_____

(f) Do you ever make use of TRAINING PACKAGES, that is, manuals, interactive videos, online learning or web-based learning resources?

_____

_____

_____

(g) Do you ever make use of DISTANCE or ON-LINE LEARNING?

_____

_____

_____

(h) Write down the PROFESSIONAL BODIES or ASSOCIATIONS to which you belong, and any Continuing Professional Development (CPD) support provided by them that you use.

_____

_____

_____

(i) Write down which COURSES and CONFERENCES you have attended in the last year.

_____

_____

_____

(j) Have you made any VISITS or STUDY TOURS in the last year?

_____

_____

_____

(k) What other ways of developing your professional knowledge have you used in the last year?

_____

_____

_____

Step 2

Now look over your answers to these questions. What sort of a picture do you get? Is CPD at the bottom of your pile of priorities or are you taking it seriously? Do you have a strategy for the future?

Keeping up to date can easily get neglected because it is not a crisis issue. Its effects are cumulative and insidious over time, the error realized only several years later. Putting time into your CPD is investing in your business – you don't get a good crop of beans without a generous investment of manure.

Now examine your answers in more detail. Many of them concern the activity of reading and using material from e-resources. Even now in the digital age this is an essential part of keeping up to date for most of us. One way to make sure that we do enough professional reading and gain most benefit from it is to read *purposefully*.

Step 3

Choose something to read – a paper, article, book chapter or web-based text. Find a time and place when you can sit down and read it.

Now review your reading using the questions in Table A4.1. There are some sample answers given, but make sure you provide your own.

Table A4.1 Reading review

Reading review questions	Some sample answers
1. For how long did I read?	e.g. – For five minutes, then I was interrupted – For half an hour, then I became bored – For ten minutes until I became exasperated with the author's views
2. Did I skim or jump forwards?	e.g. – No. I plodded through – Yes. I skimmed it first – Yes, because I couldn't understand that bit or because I knew that bit
3. Did I go back to re-read bits?	e.g. – Yes. I re-read when I couldn't understand – No. I just kept going through – Yes, because a later bit reminded me of an earlier bit so I checked back
4. Did I pause at all?	e.g. – Yes. I needed to think about an idea I had while reading – Yes. I needed a break – No. I made myself go on through
5. Did I take notes?	e.g. – Yes. Just main headings and definitions – No. I don't need to remember any of this – Yes. It's just habit with me
6. What was my purpose in reading?	e.g. – To extract practical ideas – To check my level of understanding in this field – To memorize for an examination – To decide whether to buy or borrow it.

Reviewing your reading will give you an insight into how you go about it. For example:

■ *Why* do you read (and why *don't* you)? (To glean or ransack; to escape; to meditate on, etc.)

_____

_____

_____

■ *When* do you read? (What's the best time and place for you?)

_____

_____

_____

■ *What* do you do when you get bored, lose the thread or disagree with what's written? (Give up; take a break; get angry; eat a sandwich, etc.)

_____

_____

_____

■ For *how long* can you/do you read?

_____

_____

_____

We all have our own reading patterns and preferences. Understanding your reading habits means that you will know when to read what sort of material for what purpose.

Step 4

Now choose another paper, book chapter or web-based text. Find time and space to read it. Before you start, note down the following:

■ Your purpose in reading this.

_____

_____

_____

■ How much time you have for reading.

_____

_____

_____

■ Whether or not you will take notes.

_____

_____

_____

■ Whether or not you will skim it first.

_____

_____

_____

■ Where you will do your reading.

_____

_____

_____

■   What you will do when you get bored/frustrated, etc.

_____

_____

_____

Now read. Now take the time to review again using questions in Step 3. Are your patterns becoming clearer?

Step 5

The questions in Step 1 (d) and (e) are about paper or electronic JOURNALS, MAGAZINES and NEWSLETTERS, which are an important source of up-to-date knowledge. Journal and magazine articles often lead books in opening up new knowledge by several years.

Take the lists you made in Step 1 (d) and (e) to your librarian or resource centre or to a knowledgeable friend. (If you haven't got access to any of these, that tells you something about your keeping up-to-date strategy – perhaps a first step would be to find one?)

Ask your librarian or friend to check your lists and to add to your question (d) list if possible. Is there any comment on your choices? Can you be put on a 'circulation list' for any recommended journals? There are often plenty of journals, newsletters, etc., around which don't get read by many people through not being circulated properly.

In this way, you can begin to build up a circulating network, 'papernet' or e-mailing group where you swap items of mutual interest with professional colleagues.

Step 6

Step 1, questions (f) and (g) ask about your use of PACKAGES and ON-LINE and DISTANCE LEARNING. These are increasingly available for busy managers and if you are fortunate enough to work in an organization with a training department, then this is the place to start. Make demands on your training person, but you can also try the local college or university where there may be learning resources centres.

Step 7

Question (h) in Step 1 asks about membership of PROFESSIONAL BODIES and ASSOCIATIONS. Professional bodies not only often have conferences and branch meetings where you can meet other members, but also circulate newsletters and journals. Many professional bodies encourage or even demand 'continuous professional development' and provide resources for this. You can contact them for lists of relevant packages and resources. For example, the BIM (British Institute of Management) has an excellent education information unit which will answer queries about all sorts of professional development activities.

Step 8

COURSES, CONFERENCES and VISITS are another way of updating and learning. Courses, of course, are the commonest way of keeping up to date. However, they are not designed specifically for you, and people often get sent on them rather than choosing them for themselves. Make sure you choose yourself, and know why you're going.

Step 9

Have you any other ideas for keeping up to date? As we often stress in this book, COLLEAGUES are one of the best sources of up-to-date information. To generate some fresh thoughts, go round your colleagues – how do they keep themselves up to date? And, what's new?

Step 10

A strategy for keeping up to date. After considering all these methods, how are you going to ensure you stay up to date? It is best to have a strategy which has two parts:

(a) *Choose* which methods of keeping up to date you will follow in the next, say, six months.
(b) *Plan* when, where, how, you will do these chosen activities. Use a table like that in Activity 37, *Action planning*, to help you do this. It is also a good idea to find a colleague or confidant with whom you can share your plan and review progress from time to time. This helps a lot.

Follow-up

More detailed advice on these various ways to keep yourself up to date can be found in *Key Business Concepts* by Bengt Karloff and F. Lovingsson (Routledge, 2005), which is an alphabetical guide to a large number of modern management concepts together with explanations of several well-known management models.

Steven Ten Have's *Key Management Models* (Financial Times Prentice Hall, 2002) is similar.

Professional institutions usually publish up-to-date summaries on recent trends, happenings, changes. The Chartered Institute of Management can be found at www.managers.org.uk and the Institute of Leadership and Management is at www.i-l-m.com

Internet search engines are useful, but you can be overwhelmed by irrelevance. There are websites that give guidance on how to use search engines, but these can be out of date. Search Engine Watch at http://searchenginewatch.com is currently 'live' and updated daily. It is aimed at people who really *are* interested in search engines and you can become a member and sign up for a newsletter, but it also contains information to help you use the web more efficiently.

Find a Mentor

Learning areas	**Professional knowledge:** Balanced learning habits; Proactivity

Being mentored – for a new job, a different role or a demanding task – is one of the best ways to learn. If you don't have a mentor, why not get yourself one?

Mentoring overlaps with coaching and this confusion is not helped by the fact that different definitions are used for both. Generally, whereas coaches tend to focus on specific problems or skills in the shorter term, mentors take a broader focus on the wider development of the person within a life or career. Table A5.1 below outlines these differences in more detail, contrasting the mentor role with that of the coach and the more traditional instructor.

It may be that these terms are used differently in your organization, perhaps reversing the definitions of coaching and mentoring, or using additional descriptions such as 'business mentoring' or 'life coaching'. Modify the table to suit your needs and to reflect the language used in your organization. It will then help you to understand the options and to ensure that understanding is shared with any prospective mentor.

Activity

This activity helps you to think through what you want from a mentor and get you started on a mentoring relationship.

Table A5.1 Instructor, Coach or Mentor?

Three ways of being helped to learn: Instructor, Coach or Mentor			
Dimension	Instructor	Coach	Mentor
Focus of help	Task	Job results	Development of person over career or life
Timespan	A day or two	A month to a year	Career or lifetime
Approach to helping	'Show and tell' – give supervised practice	Explore problem together and set up opportunities to try out new skills	Act as friend willing to play 'devil's advocate' – listen and question to enlarge awareness
Associated activities	Analysing task: clear instruction, practice, give feedback on results at once.	Jointly identify the problem: create development opportunity and review	Link work with other parts of life: clarify long-term aims and purpose in life
Ownership	Helper	Shared	Learner
Attitude to ambiguity	Eliminate	Use it as a challenge: as a puzzle to solve	Accept as part of life and of the world
Benefits to the business	Standard, competent performance	Goal-directed performance oriented to improvement and being creative	Conscious questioning approach to the business purpose

Adapted from the original by David Megginson.

Step 1: Who has helped me to learn?

First write down the names of the people in your life who have helped you to learn important things – go back as far as you can:

1.
2.
3.
4.
5.
etc.

Now reflect on the following questions:

■ *What do these people have in common?*

_____

_____

_____

■ *What did I receive from these people?*

_____

_____

_____

■ *What do I look for in such people?*

_____

_____

_____

Step 2: What do I need now?

Step 1 should have given you some clues about what you look for in a mentor. Perhaps this has been different for you at different times in your life? Many people look for clear advice and guidance at the start of a career, whilst later on we may look more for support and challenge of our ideas and proposals. Here are three more questions to ponder about what you want:

■ *What career/life stage are you at now?*

_____

_____

_____

■ *What sort of help for learning do you need now?*

_____

_____

_____

■ *Assuming that you have found the right person, how will you describe what you would like to receive from the relationship?*

_____

_____

_____

Step 3: Finding a mentor

A mentor may be from within your organization but can be from outside. It is usually best not to choose someone who has any line management relationship with you. Beware of any conflicts of interest in looking for a mentor, and if you choose one in your own organization it often better to look for one outside of your immediate area.

Now write down a list of all the possible people that you might choose. Don't be inhibited by thoughts about whether they will agree or not, just write down who you think you would like:

1.
2.
3.
4.
5.
etc.

If you get stuck on this list, ask a friend, or talk it over with your manager – can they suggest other good people?

Now put your list in order of priority – who is at the top?

Step 4: Making contact

Contact your No.1 person. Ask them if they can spare you half an hour to talk about your career.

Taking your courage to make contact will be the hard step for many people, but remember that you are only asking for a half hour of their time at this stage.

In your discussion with this person (and the others on your list) make sure that you cover the following:

- What sort of help you are looking for?
- When, where, for how often and for how long will you meet?
- What might be in this relationship for the other person?
- Fix the date of the next meeting.

In discussing these questions with your prospective mentor, it might be helpful to use Table A5.1 again to help check that they share the same perception of what is being described.

Good luck.

Follow-up

This activity complements many others in this book, especially Activity 25, *Be a coach!* Most of the resources for mentoring are shared with coaching as with David Megginson and David Clutterbuck's *Techniques for Coaching and Mentoring* (Oxford: Butterworth-Heinemann, 2005). The other follow-up references for Activity 25, *Be a coach!*, will also be useful.

A visit to the web will throw up thousands of offerings on mentoring. The European Mentoring and Coaching Council (EMCC), which brings together practitioners, researchers and institutions and is attempting to regulate this new profession, is a good place to start: www.emccouncil.org.

Communication Tools

Learning areas	**Professional knowledge:** Social skills: Proactivity

Do you find it easy to choose the appropriate media for communications at work?

The number and variety of communication possibilities and media increase year on year – and so do the possibilities for their inappropriate use. There are infamous examples of intimate e-mails circulating around global corporations or reaching the world's press within hours, but more mundane illustrations can be found in every workplace. People write about tricky issues when they could walk ten yards and discuss them; we call expensive meetings to transact administrative matters or hold decision-making sessions without prior agreement on agendas or circulation of relevant papers.

Do you understand which communications tool to use in what circumstances?

Activity

Step 1

Consider the ten sorts of communications situations below.

Against each one, note the medium or communications method that you would use for this situation:

Communications situations:	Appropriate communications method(s):

1. Transmission of simple data

2. Transmission of complex data

3. Making arrangements

4. Updating/keeping in touch

5. Sounding out opinions on tricky issues

6. Sorting out personal differences

7. Sorting out group conflicts

8. Making complex decisions

9. General networking

10. Communicating praise and support

Step 2

Now compare your answers with the suggestions in Table A6.1.

This matrix lists some of the main communications media across the top and the types of communication down the left-hand side.

Ticks and crosses show the recommended and non-recommended media for particular types of communication. Question marks indicate possibilities and queries.

Table A6.1   A communications matrix

	E-mail or letter	Personal phone call	One-to-one meeting	Phone or video conference	Group meeting
1. Transmission of simple data	✓	?	✕	✕	✕
2. Transmission of complex data	✓	✕	✓	?	?
3. Making arrangements	✓	✓	✕	✕	✕
4. Updating/keeping in touch	✓	✓	✓	?	?
5. Sounding out opinions	✓	✓	✓	?	?
6. Sorting out personal differences	✕	?	✓	✕	✕
7. Sorting out group conflicts	✕	✕	✕	?	✓
8. Making decisions	?	?	✓	✓	✓
9. General networking	✕	?	✓	✕	✕
10. Praise and support	✓	✓	✓	✓	✓

Step 3

How did you do? Do you think you have a good sense of what to use in which circumstances?

Some types of communication situations are fairly straightforward, e.g. 1–5 in the matrix; others are fraught with danger, e.g. 6–10 in the matrix. Take special care with these latter types.

Follow-up

No tool can do full justice to the almost infinite variety of human communications possibilities. For example, this tool does not cover those useful informal communications settings, such as the 'corridor meeting' or chatting in social spaces such as dining rooms or bars. These can be the most effective places to transact sensitive or 'unstructured' business.

The Communications Matrix tool is there to be consulted, not slavishly followed. It can be used in team meetings to agree the appropriate communications medium for any action.

Pin this above your desk and consult it whenever you are in any doubt.

Facts and Assumptions

Learning areas	**Sensitivity to events:** Self-knowledge: Social skills

We often don't bother to separate out facts from assumptions. When I enter my office in the morning, I observe facts and make assumptions. I observe that the office door is shut, but I assume much more: that the room has been cleaned; that the papers I left on my desk last night are still there; that the furniture is arranged as I left it; and so on. Assumptions nearly always outweigh observations. When I go to a meeting, I observe that certain people are present, but I make assumptions: how certain individuals will behave; how long the meeting will last; whether I will be interested or bored; and so on.

This ability to assume or predict is a valuable human skill, without which progress would be painfully slow and limited. However, sometimes when I make wrong assumptions, I act on this basis and make mistakes. If I think my ideas might be attacked at a meeting, I might decide attack first as the best form of defence. When I am attacked back my assumption is confirmed. Or is it? This is the self-fulfilling prophecy – when I make an assumption, then act on it and my action causes the effect which confirms my original but false assumption.

Another problem is that if I have already made assumptions about how things are then I may not observe certain facts that do not fit with those assumptions. This is 'selective perception'. I see what I want to see; select those things I am looking for. I go into a room looking for a book and don't notice a new furniture arrangement, because I am not looking for it.

This activity is designed to help build those mental muscles that distinguish facts from assumptions.

Activity

Step 1

Choose a person who is new to your organization, or whom you have only just met.

Step 2

Observe this person and list all those things that you can verify as *facts*: dress, appearance, expressions, behaviour and so on.

Philosophically, it is perhaps impossible to justify anything as a fact, but there are some things about which we can be relatively certain: 'He is very tall' (of a 6'3″ man), for instance. But how factual is the statement 'She is very nice'? (Even 'very tall' is subjective and may not be regarded as fact when talking about basketball players). The safest rule is to ask yourself: 'What will I accept as a fact, that is a given or commonly verifiable piece of information, in this particular situation?'

Step 3

Now make a second list of *assumptions*. These may be based upon the facts you have observed, but they should be assumptions, guesses, or predictions arising out of those facts on such matters as status, religion, likes or dislikes, personality problems, marital status, habits, opinions, attitudes and so on.

Some of these assumptions may be relatively safe: it is a fact that she is tall, therefore it is fair to assume that 'she finds the office desks uncomfortable to sit at'. Or they might be more 'risky'. 'She is tall', therefore can one assume 'her husband is tall also', or 'she feels embarrassed at being so tall'? Be honest with yourself and list all the assumptions that come to mind.

Step 4

When you have made your list of assumptions, estimate how many will be correct. If possible, check these out with the person, explaining the object of the exercise. Whatever happens you will have made a new acquaintance and possibly a friend!

What proportion of your assumptions were correct?

If you can't pluck up the courage to approach the person in question, you could ask a friend or colleague to go through the same activity and compare lists. What did you observe that your friend did not, and vice versa? What assumptions did each of you make?

Step 5

Finally, reflect on what you have learned from this activity. Write a few notes for yourself under each of the four questions below:

(a) What did you learn about the nature of 'facts'?

_____

_____

_____

(b) What did you learn about the number of assumptions you habitually make about people and situations?

_____

_____

_____

(c) Did you discover how selective your perception is?

_____

_____

_____

(d) Can you think of other situations at work where you go through similar facts – assumptions, connections?

_____

_____

_____

Follow-up

You can repeat this activity with any number of suitable people. An interesting variation is to study the next meeting or interview you attend. Draw up lists of 'facts' and 'assumptions' beforehand and observe during the event and check back on your lists afterwards. If you do this once or twice, you might be surprised at (i) how observant you're becoming; (ii) how accurate your assumptions are becoming; (iii) how cautious you are now about making assumptions!

The view that our world is 'socially constructed' has gained ground in recent years and is particularly relevant to life in organizations. Berger and Luckman's *The Social Construction of Reality* (London: Penguin, 1991) has acquired classical status since first appearing in 1966. This or Ken Gergen's *An Introduction to Social Construction* (London: Sage, 1999) will get you into the issues. More recent is Ian Hacking's *The Social Construction of What?* (Cambridge: Harvard University Press, 2000).

Fog Facts: Searching for Truth in the Land of Spin by Larry Beinhart (New York: Nation Books, 2005), is an intriguing if disturbing move into how 'facts' are constructed in the world of politics. The Taos Institute, www.taosinstitute.net, publishes guides on various aspects of social construction, and also runs workshops and other programmes.

The value of reflecting upon your own behaviour is one of the underlying themes of this book. Do this in a purposeful, insightful manner and you will get better at tuning in to situations and learning from experiences. You will develop greater self-awareness and the ability to cope with pressure and emotions.

A *Personal journal* is based on the old idea of keeping some form of diary. However, this personal journal is structured around a model of human behaviour. To get the best value from it, you need to keep the journal over at least a few weeks.

In this model there are three aspects of human behaviour:

1. *The individual's FEELINGS:* how we behave is partly determined by our feelings in a given situation. We are often only partly aware of our feelings and the effect they are having. At home and at work we often have to suppress or deny our feelings – 'the stiff upper lip' is still admired – but if you are to be in control, it is essential to be aware of your feelings and their effects.

2. *The individual's THOUGHTS and IDEAS:* in any situation we have a number of thoughts and ideas about what is happening and what we might do about it. These will be influenced by our assumptions and perceptions brought from previous experiences, which combine with any fresh thoughts and ideas triggered off by the new situation.

3. *The individual's ACTION-TENDENCIES:* we all have predispositions to certain types of action. Action-tendencies are internal motivations or forces that push individuals towards certain types of action or inaction. For example, when in strong disagreement with the views of a leader, we may nonetheless keep quiet because we fear to challenge authority. This is an action-tendency to say nothing in these situations. A different action-tendency would be a

strong need to *do* something rather than to think things out carefully – a tendency which may lead to over-hasty action.

These three elements combine to influence our behaviour. In the example above of strong disagreement with the views of a leader: my *thoughts/ideas* are that what has been said is wrong; as a result, my *feelings* are those of concern and excitement; however, owing to my other *feeling* of fear of challenging authority, my *action-tendency* is to say and do nothing.

My behaviour in this situation will depend on which of the three elements wins out. These three elements also affect each other, so that my thoughts about what is being said often depend on my feelings about the person saying it – and vice versa. Figure A8.1 shows the links between thoughts/ideas, feelings, and action-tendencies.

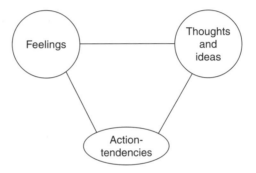

Figure A8.1   Links between thoughts/ideas, feelings and action

Although this model of behaviour is basically simple, the situations in which it operates are often very complicated. Feelings, thought/ideas and action-tendencies don't exist in a vacuum but arise in response to situational stimuli (themselves affected by previous events) and they result in behaviour, which leads to a new situation, and so on (see Fig. A8.2).

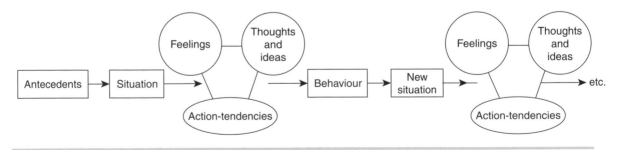

Figure A8.2   The effect situational stimuli have on feelings, thoughts/ideas and action tendencies

Activity

Keep the *Personal journal* going for a minimum of 20 entries, with at least four entries each week. A single entry might cover one specific incident, or may deal with a whole day's activities.

Some people find the *Personal journal* so useful that it becomes part of their way of life. If you keep it up for a few weeks, you will find that you are beginning to develop a 'mental' personal journal as a way of thinking.

Step 1

Take an exercise book and mark left- and right-hand pages as shown in Table A8.1. If you want more space under any heading, continue overleaf.

Table A8.1   Events and responses

What happened	My responses
	My feelings
	My thoughts and ideas
	My action-tendencies
	hence
	My behaviour

On the left-hand page write a brief description of any event that impacts on you at work. This should be factual and objective, and include a description of what led up to the situation.

Write your responses to the situation on the right-hand page. Your feelings might have changed during the event. Identify and note these. Look for feelings that were closely followed by different ones, e.g. anger often follows a feeling of being threatened.

■   Note the thoughts that you had during the situation; identify facts and assumptions.

■ Then note your action-tendencies. What other factors influenced your action (or non-action)? How did your feelings, thoughts, and action-tendencies affect each other.

■ Finally, note the effect of these elements on your behaviour – what did you actually do?

Step 2

After seven or eight entries, you can take the journal further by adding another heading of *Learning* to Table A8.1. Record your learning from these events and from your feelings, thoughts/ideas, action-tendencies, and behaviour.

Looking back over your previous journal entries, do you see any emerging patterns that tell you anything significant about yourself and other people?

Step 3

NOW WHAT?

How will you use these new insights and learning? How will you change your behaviour as a result?

Follow-up

Compile the journal over a period of time and you will become more insightful about situations and your actions in them, and you will also learn how to learn from everyday experience.

Should you become keen on journaling, there are a number of software programs that you might find of interest: www.lifejournal.com, www.splinterware. com/products/idailydiary.htm and www.davidrm.com; all provide free trial versions to test out whether they are for you.

If you'd like to step away from relying purely on writing in a journal, you may find Karen Dinino and Linda Woods' *Visual Chronicles: the No-fear Guide to Art Journals, Creative Manifestos and Altered Books* (North Light Books, 2006) opens up whole new worlds of activity for you.

Use Your Power

Learning areas	**Sensitivity to events:** Social skills: Proactivity

If the road to hell is paved with good intentions, then efforts to change often founder on the rocks of the power dynamics of organizations. We complain about 'politics' and about things happening for political reasons. The implication is that influence has been exerted and strings pulled – often in private – in a way which defeats the rational or common sense way forward.

Many of us feel wary about power, its uses and abuses. This starts at home and school and carries on into the world of work. Perhaps we have suffered from others abusing their power over us and we have all used our own power in an abusive way at some time or another. Yet very little can be done without power and indeed it is just as frequently used in a good way, to protect the weak, to influence the unwise, to achieve valued ends. Power is inherent in all situations and in all relationships. In order that it should not corrupt us, we need to understand it, how it works and how it works in us.

All organizations are political systems and all leaders and managers are political actors engaged in the 'art of the possible'. All need awareness, understanding and the ability to act effectively in this political world. This activity will help you think through the different kinds of power and the various patterns of power relationships around you.

Sources of power in organizations

Power is a loose, hard-to-define term that includes personal attributes, resources, influences and authority. Here are some sources of power, but this list is not exhaustive, so you might like to add some categories of your own:

(i) *Positional* – formal, hierarchical and status-related; position power exists when one person is 'higher' than another in a structure. Such power may carry outward signs or trappings such as expensive clothes, high salaries and designated parking spaces.

(ii) *Resources and rewards* – control of finance and other valued resources, access to premises and equipment and, especially, to people and information are often crucial in getting things done.

(iii) *Knowledge and expertise* – possessing technical ability or professional knowledge, such as that of accountants, maintenance engineers, chemists, doctors, lawyers and computer engineers, is increasingly vital in this 'information age'. As with resource power, such power is easily withheld and is often used by professionals to counter positional power.

(iv) *Personal influence* – including track record and prior achievements. Personal influence is exercised in many ways, through interpersonal skills, persuasiveness, plausibility, charm, sexual attractiveness, intellectual weight or the capacity to inspire confidence and build trust.

(v) *Networks and gossip* – within internal and external networks. 'Soft' gossipy information is often vital in terms of goings-on in the organization or the outside world. Some companies run 'soft information sessions' which link with developing environmental sensitivity and cultural awareness. The dark side of gossip is also well understood – for example, where knowledge of someone's personal life is used to damage them – but the importance of the light side is less recognized.

(vi) *Energy and stamina* – are two important qualities in getting things done. Many 'great leaders' have both of these. Staying power through stamina, adaptability, survival skills, occasional courage, steadfastness, standing by colleagues, and persistence without becoming obsessive is often underestimated, but frequently triumphs in the long run.

Activity

Use the matrix in Table A9.1 to see where the power lies in your organization – and where you stand in relation to the various kinds of power.

Table A9.1 Powerlines matrix

Sources of power \ People	Me	My boss	My staff	Colleagues	etc.
Positional					
Resources and rewards					
Knowledge and expertise					
Personal influence					
Networks and gossip					
Energy and stamina					
(Add your own)					

Step 1

Think about the kinds of power outlined above and add any others which you think we have missed or which carry special importance where you work.

Step 2

Choose a current issue or project that you are thinking about or working on. It might be your chances of being chosen to lead a particular new scheme, or it might be the general influence of your department compared with others. It helps your analysis of the situation if you think about power in relation to something specific.

Now, score yourself or your department on each type of power, using the following scale:

5 = Very strong. Well placed to deal with challenge/change/competition.
4 = Strong. Able to respond to new developments.
3 = Adequate. Will get by with a fair wind and stable conditions.
2 = Weak. Not well placed to cope with new developments.
1 = Very weak. Unable to cope with what's happening.
0 = Desperate!

Now use the same scoring system to assess the power of the other important people or groups of people in your organization. We have listed your boss, staff, colleagues, etc., but you can customize this matrix for your own purposes. For example, if you were thinking about your chances of leading a particular project then you might include the other candidates; if you were thinking about the general influence of your department then you would put in yours and all the other departments.

Step 3

Total the scores in *each vertical column* (for the matrix as it stands above, without any added factors which you may have put in, the maximum possible total for each vertical column is $6 \times 5 = 30$). Looking at the figures, ask yourself these questions:

■ Is it obvious where the power lies?

_____

_____

_____

■ Are there some big disparities of power between people or groups?

_____

_____

_____

■ Am I making best use of my strengths?

_____

_____

_____

■ How can I build up my weak areas of power?

_____

_____

_____

Now total the scores *across the columns* for each factor, and compare these with the possible totals in each direction. Ask yourself the following questions:

■ Is there a particular source of power in play here?

_____

_____

_____

■ How do I stand on that type?

_____

_____

_____

■ Is there a particularly under-used source of power here that I can bring into play?

_____

_____

_____

Step 4

Finally, make yourself an action plan to build up your weak areas of power. You can use Activity 37 *Action planning*, for this.

What you can do here depends on the resources you have available. Some sorts of power, e.g. connection power, may be easier to acquire than others – just get out more! Position power and rewards and punishment are less easy to acquire.

One good idea is to observe and then get to meet other people in your business that you see as powerful. Why do you see them in this way? Do they see themselves like this? What is the source of their power? Talk to them about it – people are often happy to talk about their strengths.

Other Activities in this book which will help you with ideas about how to build your power are 11 (*Political awareness*), 39 (*Managing upwards*) and 48 (*Managing your dependency*).

Follow-up

Power has fascinated us for millennia, and continues to do so. Analysing your situation, as a leader and manager through the activities in this book, is a simple way of doing this and may help you to use your powers more wisely. This comes partly through understanding better and also perhaps by seeing one or two things that you could do to help.

An excellent short account of organizations as political systems can be found in Chapter 6 of Gareth Morgan's classic *Images of Organisation* (2nd edition, Sage, 1997). Power is one of the core practices of leadership described especially in Chapter 5 of our own *A Manager's Guide to Leadership* (McGraw-Hill, 2004).

If you like 'no-nonsense practical tips', Jack Griffin's *How to Say it at Work: Putting Yourself Across with Power Words, Phrases, Convincing Body Language, and Communication Secrets* (NYIF, 1998) might be for you. If, on the other hand, this type of approach sticks in your craw, you might prefer Jeffery Pfeffer's *Managing with Power: Politics and Influence in Organizations* (Harvard Business School Press, 1993).

A different stance is taken by Diana Whitney and Amanda Trosten-Bloom's *Power of Appreciative Enquiry: A Practical Guide to Positive Change* (Berrett-Koehler, 2003). Here the 'power' is seen not so much as residing the individual but in a collaborative approach to getting things done.

Differences and Discrimination

The six jobs or achievements listed below on the left are those of six people listed on the right – but they have been jumbled up. Can you match them up correctly?

Job/achievement	Person
A. Orchestral musician	1. 15-year-old with cerebral palsy
B. Embroidery designer	2. Woman with serious physical disability whose height is 3′11″
C. Steeplejack	3. Profoundly deaf person
D. Fighter pilot	4. 55-year-old housewife
E. Front office receptionist for catering/tourism training organization	5. Person with two artificial legs
F. Winner of Whitbread literature prize	6. Colour-blind man

The right answers are given at the end of this Activity, but the main purpose here is for you to reflect on you reactions to the task: what went through your mind as you thought about the matching task?

Reflections of this kind can yield a lot of insight into how easily we all use preconceived notions and stereotypes to discriminate amongst and against people. Discrimination is a measure of good judgement – and weighing people up and their qualities is part of this. However, we can also make mistakes and discriminate against people on irrelevant and illegitimate grounds such as gender, sexual orientation, social class, skin colour, age, disability, religion and so on, at personal cost to them but often also at great loss to organizations. Good organizations have policies to ensure fairness and equal opportunity, but it is easy to get these things wrong when they are unfamiliar.

We have laws against certain types of discrimination, victimization and harassment, but many people are unaware that both *direct* and *indirect* discrimination are illegal. Direct discrimination means treating a person or group less favourably on gender or racial grounds than others would be treated in similar circumstances; indirect discrimination refers to unjustifiable requirements or conditions which may look equitable, but are not because particular groups can't comply with them.

Recruitment and selection are an area that worries many managers because of the costs of getting it wrong. Nothing in the law prevents an employer from choosing the best person for a job, so long as there is no discrimination because of sex, marital status or race. The activity below offers a framework to help you avoid discriminatory or exclusionary practices.

Activity

A person specification (or job specification) is the first step in a careful approach to recruitment and selection. This is created a from a job description and describes the qualities needed to do the job satisfactorily under (a) essential and (b) desirable; it can also be helpful to list (c) contraindicators: things that genuinely disqualify someone for the work. A person specification does not guarantee good selection, but it can greatly reduce errors. One of the best known formats for the person specification is the 'Seven-Point Plan' (Table A10.1).

Step 1

Specifications can become biased in subtle ways, for instance, via fallacies which may be unconscious, that certain types of work are 'more suitable' for men or women. With senior jobs, factors of social class and status can become converted into standards of appearance, education or social interests. To see how a person specification can be influenced in this way, try the following exercise:

1. Thinking of most of the *managerial and leadership* jobs in your organization, how likely are recruitment and selection to discriminate, openly or indirectly, against some categories of people by:
    - gender?
    - marital status?
    - age?
    - skin colour?
    - social class?
    - disability?

Table A10.1 The Seven-Point Plan person specification

	Essential	Desirable	Contraindicators
1. *Physical* – what does the work demand in terms of general health, physical strength or stamina, eyesight, hearing, speech, appearance?			
2. *Attainments* – education, training, experience, achievements			
3. *General intelligence* – specific indicators of reasoning ability and learning capacity			
4. *Special aptitudes* (e.g. mechanical, manipulative, mathematical, verbal/written expression, creativity)			
5. *Interests* (e.g. intellectual, practical, active, social interests relevant to work)			
6. *Disposition* – requirements in terms of working alone, getting on with others, using initiative, accepting responsibility, influencing, working under pressure			
7. *Circumstances* (e.g. travel from home, availability at certain times)			

Put your views in Table A10.2. Consider whether discrimination in recruitment and selection is likely to operates at leadership and managerial levels with regard to gender, then marital status, etc., for each of the factors in the Seven-Point Plan. If you think discrimination is likely to arise, put an 'X' in the box. Otherwise leave it blank or put in a question mark.

Table A10.2 Possible discriminatory factors

	Gender	Marital status	Age	Skin colour	Social class	Disability
1. Physical appearance						
2. Attainments						
3. General intelligence						
4. Special aptitudes						
5. Interests						
6. Disposition						
7. Circumstances						

Step 2

For each area of discrimination you have identified:

■ Who is likely to be discriminated against?

_____

_____

_____

■ How is it likely to arise?

_____

_____

_____

■ How can it be avoided?

_____

_____

_____

Step 3

In relation to your current sphere of influence, do you think discrimination affects any aspect of work? If so, what could be done to eliminate it?

Follow-up

This aspect of relationships at work may lead to difficult personal or organizational questions. But it is bigger than just about avoiding discrimination – important though that is. Learning organizations wish to make the most of all the people and their learning and a company that is discriminatory is also likely to be ineffective in terms of making the most of its resourceful humans.

There are many sources of useful reading and information in this area. A very readable, short guide to the concept of 'managing diversity' and to the basic good practices involved is Linbert Spencer's *The Diversity Pocketbook* (Alresford: Management Pocketbooks, 2004). A more detailed treatment can be found in *Race, Politics and Social Change* by Solomos and Back (London: Routledge, 1995) which provides insights into the political and practical problems surrounding the management of equal opportunities.

The Chartered Institute of Personnel and Development (CIPD) publishes a number of items on various aspects of diversity. Rajvinder Kandola and Joanna Fullerton's *Managing the Mosaic: Diversity in Action* (2nd edition, London: CIPD, 1998) is something of a classic. And if you want a set of tools that shows you how to ensure that diversity – the vision and policies – gain organization acceptance and form part of the overall strategic framework that supports long-term business goals, then £300 for Pearn Kandola's *Managing Diversity* (2nd edition, London: CIPD, 2006) might well be a useful investment. The CIPD is also a useful source of information about equal opportunities policy and practice: 151 The Broadway, London SW19 1JQ, tel. 020 8612 6200; www.cipd.co.uk.

More specifically, *Pride Against Prejudice: Transforming Attitudes to Disability* by Jenny Morris (Women's Press, 1991) remains a powerful and useful text, as does Rohan Collier's *Combating Sexual Harassment in the Workplace* (Open University Press, 1995). A more recent publication is *Bullying and Sexual Harassment,* by Tina Stephens and Jane Hallas (Chandos Publishing, 2006).

In addition to the CIPD mentioned above, other useful contact include:

(i)   Royal Association for Disability and Rehabilitation (RADAR), 12 City Forum, 250 City Road, London EC1V 8AF, tel. 020 7250 3222; www.radar.org.uk.

(ii) Royal National Institute for the Blind (RNIB), 105 Judd Street, London WC1H 9NE, tel. 020 7388 1266; www.rnib.org.uk.

(iii) Royal Association for Deaf People (RAD), Walsingham Road, Colchester, Essex CO2 7BP, tel. 01206 509509; www.royaldeaf.org.uk.

(iii) Equal Opportunities Commission (EOC), Arndale House, Arndale Centre, Manchester M4 3EQ, tel. 0161 838 8312; www.eoc.org.uk.

(iv) The Commission for Racial Equality (CRE), St Dunstan's House, 201–211 Borough High Street, London SE1 1GZ, tel. 020 7939 0000; www.cre.gov.uk.

(v)   Disability Rights Commission, DRC Helpline, FREEPOST MID02164, Stratford upon Avon CV37 9BR, tel. 08457 622 633; www.drc-gb.org.

Answers to matching task

A = 3 (Evelyn Glennie)
B = 6*
C = 4*
D = 5 (Sir Douglas Bader)
E = 2*
F = 1 (Christy Nolan, *Damburst of Dreams*)

* Private individuals known to the authors.

Political Awareness

Learning areas	**Sensitivity to events:** Social skills: Proactivity

Leaders and managers are increasingly expected to be political sensitive and aware. We have lots of words to describe this ability – we call it *nous* or being *streetwise, savvy, clued-up, on the ball* – and recognize it in people who somehow know who to talk to, who to agree with and who to disagree with. We also recognize the political innocents among us who seem to have very little idea of what is going on. However knowledgeable or skilled you are in your own field, you can't get things done without knowing how the organization works.

Another problem is how to act with political awareness *and* with integrity. Many people enjoy some gameplaying as part of the fun of being in the organization. But those for whom the game becomes the main issue we might call clever, but never wise. While innocents can exhibit a kind of wisdom, we would only use the word wise of someone who (a) knows what is going on and (b) bases their actions on the longer term perspective based on personal values rather than short-term political advantage.

This activity does not guarantee wisdom, but it might help you to become a little more streetwise around your organization.

Activity

Step 1

First, think of a change that you want to make – small or large. Even small changes – such as in paperwork systems, furniture layout, meal times and so on – will illustrate the effects of power and politics very nicely. However, make sure the change is important to you and that you do intend to make it.

Step 2

(i) Using the *Political mapping: Who's who?* worksheet in Table A11.1, list in the left-hand column all the people and groups who are involved in making the change or who will be affected by it.

(ii) Now list the *interests* of each of these people or groups in the centre column. In thinking of interests it is useful to consider:

- ■ *vested* interests – salary, resources, career prospects, territory, advantages, perks, etc.
- ■ *ideological* interests – political or philosophical commitments
- ■ *self*-interests – personal values, sense of personal and professional identity.

(iii) Third, note in the right-hand column what you see as each person or group's main sources of power. One classification of power sources is:

1. position
2. resources and rewards
3. knowledge and expertise
4. personal influence
5. networks and gossip
6. energy and stamina.

(You can find explanations of these in Activity 9, *Use your power.*)

Table A11.1   **Micro-political mapping: Who's who?**

People/Group	Interests	Power sources

Having listed all those involved, their interests and sources of power, to which of these do you need to pay special attention?

If you have a long list, you may feel that it would be better to let sleeping dogs lie. A well-known problem with analysis is that it can lead to paralysis. However, that is not the intention here: the aim is to empower you to act with political awareness and integrity! The next step should help you to move on.

Step 3

Now consider the *orientation* of each of your people or groups to the change you have in mind. The worksheet in Table A11.2 has two dimensions:

(i) Support/resist – is the person or group supportive of or resistant to the change?
(ii) Power – does the person or group have high or low power in this situation?

This gives four obvious locations:

Powerful and supportive	Powerful and resistant
Weak and supportive	Weak and resistant

Now mark your people or groups on the worksheet. You can assign them simply to one of the quadrants or you can grade them carefully with regard to the vertical and horizontal scales.

Table A11.2 Micro-political mapping: change orientation

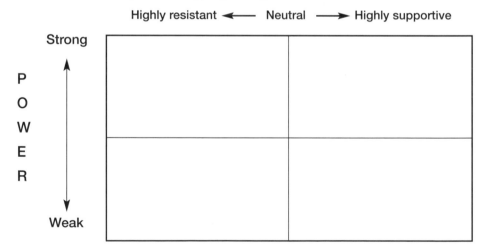

Step 4

How does your chart look? Does it show a critical mass of support for your change or solid ranks of resistance against it?

In the latter case, should you rethink your ideas or reconsider your plans?

If, as often, the picture is more evenly balanced, what could you do to increase support for your change? Can you approach individuals or groups to:

- Find out why the resisters are resisting? Do they understand fully the proposed change? What are their objections? Is there anything they would like which would change their positions?
- Ask powerful supporters to approach powerful resisters to try to 'get them on board' or at least to reduce their resistance?
- Help those who are supportive but weak become more powerful? Perhaps the people in this quadrant could be brought together to reduce isolation and develop a sense of joint identity? Can they be encouraged to speak up at meetings? Can their status be raised in any way?

Follow-up

Power is one of the core practices of leadership described especially in Chapter 5 of our own *A Manager's Guide to Leadership* (McGraw-Hill, 2004). Some people find it hard to understand why such thinking is useful in preparing to make changes. Nicolo Machiavelli is often invoked with his ruminations on 'whether it is better to be loved than to be feared' and his exhortations to 'be like a lion and a fox' (presumably, to be able to be forthright and honest as well as sly and devious). Some organizations do bear a passing resemblance to the Medici court, and if you happen to work in one of these then perhaps 'The Prince' is still as good a guide as any – or if you prefer an updated equivalent try Michael Arthur Ledeen's *Machiavelli on Modern Leadership* (St Martin's Press, 2000).

However, most of the time, organizations employ manners and methods which have moved on in the last 500 years. Many, especially those which employ many professional communities of practice, are complicated to lead and to manage because all changes to the existing order tend to require a process of continuous negotiation. 'Micro-political mapping' will help you to become that bit more knowing and it should make your change efforts that bit more successful. 'In being political we walk the tightrope between advocating our own position and yet not increasing resistance against us by our actions'– thus Peter Block opens his *The Empowered Manager: Positive Political Skills at Work* (Jossey-Bass, 1991), a well respected work.

'Micro-political mapping' is taken from Mike Pedler and Kath Aspinwall's *Perfect plc?: The Purpose and Practice of Organizational Learning* (McGraw-Hill, 1996), which will be helpful to anyone thinking about change in complex organizations. Finally, Chapter 6 of Gareth Morgan's *Images of Organisation* (3rd edition, Sage, 2006) is the best short account of organizations as political systems and is invaluable background reading.

Credulous Listening

Learning areas	**Sensitivity to events:** Social skills: Balanced learning habits

"If you want to know something about a person, ask – they just might tell you"
George Kelly

George Kelly published his ideas almost 50 years ago, and the implications are still emerging. Kelly believed that although the world is real and not a figment of our imaginations, each individual tries for themselves to grasp and make sense of the world and only ever partly succeeds. We all construct our own understandings or *personal constructs* which are each person's unique ways of understanding his or her world. We have common understandings with others, but we only if we have a sense of their value systems as well as our own.

Helen Jones, who works with Kelly's ideas, places great importance on *credulous listening*, which implies:

(i) believing that what the other person says is true for them; and
(ii) suspending our own ideas and constructs in order to understand the *personal constructs* of the other person.

Many of us find this difficult. In talking with others, we often internally translate what they are saying so that it matches our own ideas. Sometimes our own ideas, prejudices and assumptions get in the way so much that we think, 'Why is she telling me this?' or 'Here he goes again!', so that we can hardly hear what they say at all. To deal with this problem it is necessary to become – at least for a time – a *credulous listener*.

Activity

Step 1

Choose a time when you know that you are going to be meeting with someone whose ideas, values or beliefs you find difficult.

Decide that you will listen credulously to everything that they are going to say – yes, everything!

This means that you will be accepting that what they say is *true for them*.

Step 2

Because credulous listening is difficult, set yourself a target, say, to listen credulously for 20 or 30 minutes. If possible, take a break at this point in order to jot down their ideas and perhaps to reflect them back to the person. Take the chance to check out whether you have fully understood the meanings and implications which the words have for the other person.

To listen credulously to another you also have to listen to yourself. When you 'hear' yourself becoming incredulous, and in order to suspend these views, say to yourself something like: 'What this person is saying is true for them, I don't have to agree or disagree, but just listen and try to understand'.

If you do any interviewing or counselling you will have had a taste of this experience. Here the task is to enable the other person to tell *their* point of view, *their* taste, *their* perceptions. Yet, even in this formal situation, it can be very hard not to impose your own construction of events on what is being said, and reveal this in your tone of voice, raised eyebrows, selective questions and so on.

Step 3

How did you do?

Did you really listen credulously?

Do you understand that person's view of the world better?

If you can answer 'Yes' to these questions, then give yourself a pat on the back. You have given another person that all too rare experience of being really listened to, and you might well have learned something new for yourself. Through credulous listening we escape the limits of our own thoughts and imaginations and gain access to a wider world.

Follow-up

Practising credulous listening is one of the most valuable skills that you are likely to find in this book. You can practice this on your own by doing some *credulous reading*. This involves the two processes – loosening and tightening – that Kelly made central to his idea of people as experimenters continually testing their understandings of the world. Loosening (exploring and trying out ideas) and tightening (choosing options and making things happen) are reciprocal and repeated activities that are core to the learn process.

Next time you're reading a book, think about the *way* you're reading. Here are two possible extreme positions:

'Being taken over' by the story, being enamoured, getting lost in it (loosening)	'Reading for a purpose', ransacking the text for a specific end; instrumental; judgemental (tightening)

Depending on *how* you read it, you will take different things from the book. It's the same as with people.

George Kelly's *The Psychology of Personal Constructs* (London: Routledge, 1991; a reprint of his 1955 volumes) is heavy going, and also out of print. Good introductions to the ideas are Fay Fransella's *The Essential Handbook of Personal Construct Psychology* (Chichester: Wiley, 2005) and Trevor Butt's *Understanding People* (Palgrave Macmillan, 2003).

The Saturated Life

Learning areas	**Emotional resilience:** Self-knowledge

The issue

There are few people doing management and leadership work who do not feel busy, stretched and overloaded. We are overloaded not just by tasks and demands on our time, but by stimuli, information, data – messages of all kinds.

Kenneth Gergen coined the phrase 'the saturated self' to label this phenomenon in which our selves are battered by demands to be and do things. The information/message overload does not just create work in itself; it makes demands on our emotions, sense of self and identity.

Messages give us information and make demands on us to respond, to do something. They communicate other peoples' expectations of us including telling us how to be (as in advertising). 'Active load' consists of messages passed directly to us: information, knowledge, expectations, response demands; 'Passive load', like passive smoking, is advertising, publicity, propaganda and unsolicited communications of all kinds.

The load problem is to do with how much we can cope with in processing terms. But more than that, these are demands on our energy, emotions, sense of self, image and reputation. The active and passive load can exert many conflicting demands that exhaust us, cause us to distort things and become internalized as problems.

Activity

Step 1: Getting the feel of your message load

Make some notes on your active and passive message loads now, compared with some time ago – when you were growing up, or starting work. Think of your active load now: e-mails, phone messages, phone calls, paperwork and meetings. Think of your passive load – news, advertising, hoardings, labels, noticeboards.

	Active load	Passive load
Now		
Before		

Step 2: Exploring your message load

Think about the following, and write a few notes on them:

(a) What are the times and where are the places where your 'message load' comes to you?

_____

_____

_____

(b) Do you stimulate or inhibit the message load that you get? Are you selective about how you do this?

_____

_____

_____

(c) Some people are 'stimulus addicts' – they set themselves up for a continuous flow of messages to save thinking, addressing priorities, facing up to problems. Can you detect any signs of this in yourself?

_____

_____

_____

Step 3: Things to do about it

Consider your answers to the following questions:

(a) What do you do to manage the active message demand on you? Do you have an approach to influencing the sources of messages to give you just what you want, not too much not too little?

_____

_____

_____

(b) Do you manage the passive message demand on you? Do you limit the amount of advertising, general news, notices that you allow to take your attention? How?

_____

_____

_____

(c) Do you create breathing spaces, places and times where you are not exposed to messages, have time to reflect, get back in touch with yourself and priorities? When?

_____

_____

_____

(d) Or the other side of this coin, do you limit the times and places that messages can get to you, and control when and where you deal with them? How?

_____

_____

_____

(e) Do you have a way of being selective about the messages that reach you, and the degree of urgency with which they do so? How?

_____

_____

_____

(f) Are you proactive in arranging for your messages to be at the right level of summarization for you, e.g. executive summaries rather than full reports, headline statistics not masses of data?

_____

_____

_____

(g) Can you be comfortable 'not knowing' about some things – trusting others to deal with them, or tell you if anything exceptional or unusual comes up?

_____

_____

_____

(h) Can you avoid just being a messenger – passing on information that does not really have to come through you – by arranging for it to pass you by and go directly to where it is needed?

_____

_____

_____

(i) In some workplaces people seem to get into competitive and dysfunctional games of swamping and drowning each other in messages – consciously or unconsciously. Are you caught up in this? How can you avoid it?

_____

_____

_____

(j) Do you take enough time to 'collect yourself and your thoughts' – to work out what you are doing and what information you actually need, as opposed to get?

_____

_____

_____

(k) Do you consider the message load on others – identifying and understanding their problems and situations, and what you do to increase or decrease it?

_____

_____

_____

(l)   There are many positive aspects of living in an information/demand-rich world – are you skilled in using it to find out what you want, rather than being swamped by it?

_____

_____

_____

Follow-up

The core idea for this activity is in Kenneth Gergen's *The Saturated Self: Dilemmas of Identity in Contemporary Life* (Basic Books, HarperCollins, 1991).

Activity 14

Decision Making

Making decisions is a critical aspect of the leader or manager's job. Robert Townsend said that perhaps 40% of the decisions he made as Managing Director of Avis turned out to be wrong in some way. Most important, though, he made them.

So, first-class leaders might average 50% or 60% correct decisions. (It takes a first-class leader to admit this.) All decisions are hedged with uncertainty – otherwise they would not be decisions – yet we humans have a remarkable facility for 'rationalizing' and justifying our actions, and do this for ourselves even when not called to account by others. If we did less of this we would recognize how many of our decisions turned out to be wrong, and therefore be prepared accordingly. An initial decision on a new project can spawn many more crisis/decision points as it gets under way.

Broadly speaking, there are two ways of making decisions:

- A 'rational' process of planning: specifying alternatives, criteria and payoff probabilities until the 'correct' solution emerges (Type A).
- Following 'hunches' or intuition: taking action without planning because action creates information and information reduces uncertainty (Type B).

Depending on our training and personality, most of us use one of these modes more than the other – even to the exclusion of the other. This is perhaps natural, but it limits our capacity for meeting different kinds of decisions. Complex decisions may demand the use of both modes at different times.

Activity

Below are some sample decisions. Although some may be complex, we shall treat them as simple and say that one mode of decision making is more suitable than the other.

Step 1

Read each sample decision and decide whether it is Type A (rational) or Type B (intuitive):

1. Getting yourself from your place of work to a meeting in another specific location.
2. Being dropped anywhere in the country, without knowing where, with £10, and the task of getting home. Imagine yourself standing in open country surrounded by a light fog.
3. Choosing the means of communicating some minor redundancies in the company, given a 48-hour deadline and a partly unionized workforce.
4. Selecting an incentive payment scheme for a work area where workloads are extremely variable and where payment has previously been on a flat rate.
5. Deciding how to approach your boss about a favour you want and knowing that he or she can be very moody and changeable.
6. Deciding how to run a particular appraisal interview.

You might well say that you would use both decision types as appropriate. We say that in *broad terms* the decisions split as shown in Table A14.1.

Table A14.1   A = rational; B = intuitive

Decision	Type
1	A
2	B
3	A
4	A
5	B
6	B

Step 2

Your choice of decision type has a very marked effect on how you act when faced with a particular problem. Think about and jot down the steps you would take on decisions 1 and 2 above. Then answer the following:

(a) Are your notes very similar for decisions 1 and 2, or very different?

(b) Which did you find easier: 1 or 2?

You probably found decision 1 easier to tackle.

Decision 1 is Type A (rational); the goal is clear and there are relatively well-structured alternatives. Therefore, a rational decision is possible by sifting the alternatives against the criteria and choosing appropriately as in Table A14.2.

Table A14.2

Problem-solving stages	Decision 1
1. Analysis the problem in terms of: (a) how things are; (b) how I want things to be	1. I am at work and I want to get to the meeting in London
2. Specify *your objective* in terms of the change you want to bring about (i.e. A→B)	2. (Already stated in 1 above)
3. Specify the alternative courses of action open to you to achieve the objective	3. Go by: – car – train – taxi – bus – aeroplane – get a lift from a colleague
4. Specify the *criteria* (i.e. what characteristics must a course of action have to achieve your objective)	4. – I need to be there by 10 a.m. and I don't want to stay overnight (before or after) – It must not cost more than £50 – It would be useful to be able to read the papers for the meeting on the journey – I need to be fresh on arrival
5. Choose the alternative which best meets the criteria	5. The train meets the criteria. The car fails on criteria three and four; the taxi on criterion two; the bus is noisy and fails on four; there is no plane until 10 a.m. and this fails on criterion one; travelling with a colleague is possible but would hinder criterion three
6. Implement the alternative	6. Catch the train
7. Check whether you have achieved your goal and, if not, return to 1	7. Did you get to the meeting on time and fresh?

Decision 2 does not lend itself to such an analysis. There is a clear goal: you want to get home, but you have no idea where you are and there is much more uncertainty in this situation than in decision 1 with no clearly structured alternative actions open to you.

With this lack of information, the value of planning is limited. In well-structured situations, *planning* can usefully precede *action*; in unstructured situations, where uncertainty predominates, it is better to get into action quickly because *action generates information*. In conditions of uncertainty, *action has to precede planning*, because it generates the information required for planning. Or, to put it another way, the first objective in uncertain situations is to generate information. You choose an action to this end and pursue it until further information is obtained, at which point planning may be appropriate.

In decision 2, an intelligent action is to walk in a fixed direction (not in a circle) because this would give you maximum chance of uncovering information: a stream, a path, a road, a clearing in the mist, etc. If you find a path then you clearly have a much more structured choice – whether to follow it and, if so, in which direction. As paths always lead from one place to another, you will tend to follow it in the hope of finding out where you are, i.e. to generate more information. Eventually, you will generate enough information to know what kind of a problem you have in getting home, and what the alternatives are. You are then back in a rational decision 1 process.

In decision 5 there are no obvious alternative courses of action because the boss is *unpredictable*. A carefully planned strategy could be disastrous because plans possess momentum that is hard to modify. The best approach might be to stay neutral until their behaviour provides clues to their mood, then you can plan on your feet what action to take.

Decision 6 is a similar situation unless you regard it as a one-way process – in which case you can adopt a 'rational' approach without the need to generate information about the other person's feelings and views. Yet most interpersonal situations demand the *action before planning* approach and this is the area of decision making that creates many problems for managers. Those who are able to suspend their planning skills to generate sufficient information about alternatives and criteria *according to other people* will usually make better decisions. They are more 'socially skilled' than managers who impose a previously-planned 'rational' decision upon others.

To summarize: use a rational process for well-structured situations and an *action before planning* approach where there is little or no information (you must first be able to admit/recognize that there is little or no information). In uncertain situations, the following advice is useful:

■ Regard obtaining information as an objective in itself.
■ Be prepared to get quickly into action of a kind that generates information.

■ Be prepared to go through many cycles of action ——➤ information ——➤ planning ——➤ action.

This is also a rational decision-making process once you recognize its cyclical nature; the need to start with information-getting as the objective; the need to move into action on an experimental basis.

Step 3

As a final test of your understanding of the difference between the two approaches to decision making, reflect upon a recent or current decision and ask yourself:

■ Has 'information-getting' been an objective?

■ Has there been enough experimental action?

■ Have I picked up all the information available from experimental action and from elsewhere?

■ Have I analysed the available information carefully and did it result in improved understanding?

Follow-up

There are many books on decision making, as a visit to amazon.co.uk will confirm. John Adair's *Decision Making and Problem Solving* (London: CIPD, 1999) is a relatively recent book by a long-standing practitioner, and another very practical introduction to techniques of decision making is *The Decision-making Pocketbook*, by Neil Russell-Jones (Alresford: Management Pocketbooks, 2000).

You might also want to consider some of software packages. Spreadsheet programs allow for easy 'what if' or sensitivity projections and forecasts, while project planning packages enable you to plan your own critical paths. There are many books on using spreadsheets and databases – it's hard to make a specific recommendation as these are constantly being updated and depend very much on your own preferred style. *Mastering Spread-sheets and Forecasts* by

Malcolm Secrett (London: Financial Times Prentice Hall, 1999) is a simple, step-by-step guide to computerized budgeting, and *Data Analysis and Business Modelling with Excel* by W. Winston (Redmond: Microsoft Press, 2004) helps to do what its title suggests.

All of the above tend to the linear and rational. In these days of chaos and fractals, alternative approaches are appearing. An excellent introduction to these is Edwin Olson and Glenda Eoyang's *Facilitating Organizational Change: Lessons from Complexity Science* (San Francisco: Jossey-Bass Wiley, 2001).

Role Set Analysis

Learning areas	**Analytical skills:** Situational facts

The concept of role has a central place in organizational theories. Leadership roles, decision-making roles and supervisory roles are just a few examples of the frequent use we make of this term.

The term is borrowed from the stage where it is an act or a series of actions. In performing the life roles of child, wife or husband, parent or neighbour, whilst we remain ourselves, our behaviour is largely determined by the role we occupy at a given time. Indeed, if we don't appropriately alter behaviour in these situations we run into trouble. Errors of this sort – as in speaking to your partner as you might to your young child – are a form of role conflict.

This conflict happens because all roles carry expectations about behaviour. Attached to each role are the other people who make up a role network. Role conflict occurs when:

- Two people make opposing or conflicting demands on the role-holder, e.g. the boss who wants the manager to discipline his staff who, in turn, want protection from the boss.
- We occupy several different roles in quick succession and the demands of one conflict with those of another, e.g. work roles conflicts with partner and parent roles when you need to work late or at the weekend.
- Roles carry expectations which conflict with personal values, e.g. as a senior manager I have to overlook certain commercial practices, such as giving inducements to secure certain contracts, which I disapprove of ethically.

Role conflict is a major cause of workplace stress, and to avoid stress, role relationships have to be managed like any other part of the job. This activity will help you to think about your role as a leader or manager and:

- clarify your position within your organization
- establish what demands and expectations are made on you
- identify possible and actual areas of role conflict which helps to reduce the stress
- lay the foundations for improving your performance – at work and at home.

Activity

Step 1

Take a large sheet of paper and draw a circle in the middle to represent the role you occupy at work. Label this circle, e.g. 'Office Manager' (J. Brown). Next, draw smaller circles around the centre circle to represent all the 'significant others' in the role network of the office manager. These are all the people who make demands upon and have expectations about the role. In addition, the role has reciprocal expectations and makes demands upon them.

You can show the strength of particular links by making these roles nearer or further from the centre. Those people with whom you have daily contact probably make more demands and have more expectations of you than those you meet weekly. The role network for the office manager might look like Fig. A15.1.

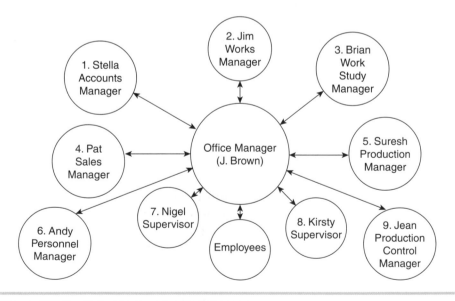

Figure A15.1   Role of network office manager

Step 2

Once you have completed your role network diagram, ask someone else their views about it.

■ Have you included all the significant role relationships?

■ How different is your role network from others around you?

■ How does it feel to be the 'person-in-the-middle' making and meeting all these demands?

Step 3

Once you have included all the vital role relationships for your job, take another sheet of paper and make a chart like that in Table A15.1. On the left-hand side

Table A15.1   Analysis of expectations

Role	Their demands/ expectations of me	My expectations/ demands of them	Possible conflict areas
Supervisors (2)	1. Fair allocation of work 2. Support for their actions 3. Personal support (e.g. to listen and be available) 4. To provide resources to allow them to get the work done 5. Set realistic work targets	1. Achieve set work targets 2. Deal with most grievances and people problems 3. Keep me informed about a variety of things (e.g. current workloads, supply of materials, personnel issues) 4. Be proactive – set own work targets in consultation with me	Supervisor actions especially on discipline and grievances are not always consistent with company personnel policy Supervisors dependent on me – will not take responsibility
Employees (16)	1. To treat them fairly 2. To arbitrate over matters of disagreement with supervisors	1. To work well and achieve work targets	Cannot satisfy both employees' demands on me to arbitrate *and* supervisors' demands for support of their actions

AND SO ON …

put all those roles that make demands upon your role and fill in across the three columns: 'Their demands/expectations of me'; 'My expectations/demands of them' and 'Possible conflict areas'.

Step 4

How can this role chart help?

■ First, are you aware of all the demands and expectations of you? Are you sure you have them right?
If you are in any doubt about what is expected of you by some other role holder, use this question to go and check this out.

■ Second, does your perception of what they want from you fit with theirs? If you asked them, would they agree with what you'd written?
Again, the obvious way to check this out is to ask – wherever you are in doubt.

■ Third, what conflicts appear – between different expectations, between you personally and your role demands, etc.?

How can you resolve or cope with these? Sometimes the answer is fairly simple. For example, on the office manager's role chart (Table A15.1), the first conflict area – 'Supervisor actions especially on discipline and grievances are not always consistent with company personnel policy' – may point to a training need.

Follow-up

The Wisdom of Teams by Jon Katzenbach and Douglass Smith (Maidenhead: McGraw-Hill, 1998) is a very useful book for teambuilding with your role set.

Rosemary Stewart's *Managing Today and Tomorrow* (Basingstoke: Palgrave Macmillan, 1993) offers ways of thinking about the discretion you have in the managerial role and how this is affected by your role set. Meredith Belbin's *Management Teams: Why They Succeed or Fail* (2nd edition, Oxford: Elsevier Butterworth-Heinemann, 2004) extends his earlier ideas on roles and their interaction to show how you can get the best from a team.

Planning Change

Analytical skills: Proactivity

This activity contains the famous planning tool *Force Field Analysis* and is credited to Kurt Lewin, whose 'field theory' described a field of forces or pressures acting on any particular event. In this view, all situations can be seen as being in temporary equilibrium, with the forces acting to change the situation being balanced by the forces acting to resist the change (Fig. A16.1).

This view of events is a dynamic one, which sees all things, including especially social situations, as temporary states of balance. It offers the leader the opportunity to see situations as potentially changeable: if the different forces can be identified, then it may be possible to change their direction or strength.

Use this activity for a problem that has been worrying you and which seems intractable. The Force Field Analysis will make the options clearer and bring a vague problem into focus and be more 'do-able'.

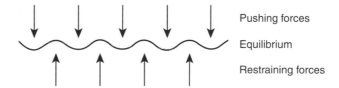

Figure A16.1   Force Field Analysis

Activity

Apply Force Field Analysis to a particular problem or situation that is currently facing you and that you would like to change or influence.

Step 1

Choose a problem and write it down.

It must be a real one that concerns you right now. The example given in Figure A16.2 is that of a manager worried by a rise in errors on their section.

Step 2

Define the problem in specific terms.

■   Who is involved?

■   What is the magnitude of the problem?

■   What other factors bear on the situation?

For example, errors have risen in Section B over the last six months.

Errors were averaging 5% but have now doubled to 10%. Relevant factors may include a recent influx of new staff and a change in incentives to increase output.

Step 3

Now state specifically how you would like to influence or change the situation.

Make this as measurable as possible; set a clear target and know when you are reaching it. For example, 'I aim to reduce the error rate to 6%'.

Step 4

Looking at the problem as a temporary equilibrium held in place (for the moment) by pushing and restraining forces, list these forces operating on your problem.

(a) What are the forces that would move the present situation towards my goal? (PUSHING FORCES)

(i)

(ii)

(iii)

(iv)

(v)

(vi)

(b) What are the forces resisting or stopping the situation approaching my goal? (RESTRAINING FORCES)

(i)

(ii)

(iii)

(iv)

(v)

(vi)

For example, on the problem of reducing Department B's error rate:

(a) PUSHING FORCES (to reduce error rate):
  (i) manager's desire to lower the rate
  (ii) company's concern at its image
  (iii) staff concern at loss of earnings
  (iv) customer complaints
  (v) planned training courses for new staff.
(b) RESTRAINING FORCES (tending to increase error rate):
  (i) influx of untrained staff
  (ii) company pressure for increased output;
  (iii) new incentive scheme
  (iv) casual attitude of younger staff concerning general behaviour and discipline
  (v) resentment of some older staff at being pushed on output.

Make sure you have listed all the forces operating on the problem. Have you included especially:

■ the motivations of individuals and groups involved?
■ organizational policies and procedures?
■ outside forces operating in the work environment?

Step 5

When you have all the relevant forces listed, rank their power as being HIGH, MEDIUM or LOW
  Do this for both PUSHING and RESTRAINING FORCES.

Step 6

Now diagram the two sets of forces as in the example in Fig. A16.2, using the length of the arrows to indicate the magnitude of the force. In the example, the manager's desire to reduce the rate is a HIGH power PUSHING force, whereas the casual attitude of younger staff is a MEDIUM power RESTRAINING force.

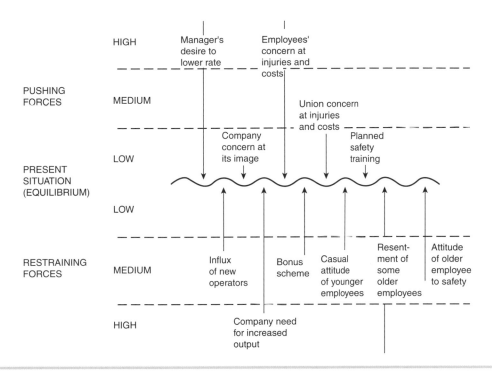

Figure A16.2 Force field analysis

Step 7

Now prepare a strategy for changing the situation.

Remember:

(a) *That if you increase the PUSHING forces that this often creates **greater** resistance in people and in systems.*

(b) *Change is most easily accepted when it requires a minimum of effort and disruption.*

Can you:

1. Maintain PUSHING forces, but reduce any of the RESTRAINING forces?
2. Find new PUSHING forces?
3. If you must PUSH more, choose forces that do not increase resistance?
4. Divert any RESTRAINING forces to new targets or in new directions?
5. Are you sure that it is not one of your PUSHING forces which created the problem in the first place? Would a reduction in this PUSH also reduce the RESTRAINING force?

Your strategy should plan some action steps in sequence, with rough timings and the resources you will need at each stage, particularly those people who can help.

It is very helpful to have sub-goals along the way to check your progress (a single far-off goal can be daunting). The lessons in Activity 14, *Decision making*, about action creating information for further planning will also be useful here.

Follow-up

As an analysis tool, Force Field Analysis can be used to examine any problem situation. More than just a technique, it is a way of seeing situations as being only in temporary equilibrium and amenable to change.

For bringing about change for a whole systems approach, see *Leading Change: A Guide to Whole Systems Working* by Margaret Attwood, Mike Pedler, Sue Pritchard and David Wilkinson (Bristol: The Policy Press, 2003). Similarly, *The Change Handbook* edited by Peggy Holman and Tom Devane (San Francisco: Berrett Koehler, 1999) has 18 chapters on how to bring about change in communities and organizations from a whole systems perspective.

A much shorter book is David Casey's *Managing Learning in Organisations* (Maidenhead: Open University Press, 1993), which is a fine distillation of 30 years' experience of working with change for individuals, teams and organizations. Finally, Esther Cameron and Mike Green provide a good summary in *Making Sense of Change Management: A Complete Guide to the Models, Tools and Techniques of Organizational Change* (London: Kogan Page, 2004).

Activity 17

Catastrophic Contingencies

Learning areas	**Analytical skills:** Creativity: Emotional resilience: Proactivity: Self-knowledge

Many leaders and managers, faced with complex decisions, find themselves blocked in by the fear of 'what if ...?' Faced with uncertainty, doubt and the possibility of a bad, even catastrophic, consequence to our action, we tend towards stress and the inability to act.

This activity is designed to help you overcome this kind of blockage.

Activity

Step 1

Next time you are faced with a difficult problem, involving uncertainty, risk, or doubt – write down, first, the various courses of action open to you. Then list the worst possible things that could happen if everything went wrong.

What are the worst catastrophes that could occur?

Step 2

Take each catastrophe in turn and imagine that it really has happened. How do you feel in this disastrous situation? Is it so awful, or were your fears exaggerated? Again, imagining that it has already happened: What are you going to do now? From this catastrophic situation what are your plans? How are you going to cope with it? What could you have done to lessen its bad effects? (Imagine yourself saying 'things wouldn't be so bad if only I ...'.)

Step 3

When you have answered these questions, you will probably find that:

(a) Many possible catastrophes are not really as bad as your first, unconsidered fears.
(b) You have identified some of the plans and actions that you can implement to lessen either the probability of the catastrophe's occurrence or the severity of its effects.
(c) You have prepared some contingency plans for coping with the catastrophe should it occur. These will be helpful in themselves and, by reducing the ambiguity and helplessness of the situation, you will have lessened your fear of it.

You should now be able to overcome the blockage and make your decisions.

Follow-up

When drawing up your contingency plans, Activities 16 (*Planning change*) and 37 (*Action planning*) will be helpful.

At the corporate level, this is similar to scenario planning, described in Gill Ringland's *Scenario Planning* (2nd edition, Chichester: Wiley, 2006). You start by thinking of alternative economic, social and political changes that might occur – for example, what if the oil price were to rise ten-fold? What if all our assets in a certain country were nationalized? You then estimate the effect of these changes on your business, and make contingency plans accordingly.

Again at a corporate level, the *Manager's Guide to Contingency Planning for Disasters*, by Kenneth Myers (New York: Wiley, 1999) projects an optimistic view of the ability to make contingency plans for disasters. James Ogilvy's *Building Better Futures: Scenario Planning as a Tool for Social Creativity* (Oxford: Oxford University Press, 2002) shows how we can create change in our own communities and neighbourhoods.

At the team level, you can find 'witty and enlightening accounts of team disasters and how they could have been avoided' in *Team Traps: Survival Stories and Lessons from Team Disasters, Near-misses, Mishaps, and Other Near-death Experiences*, by Steven R. Rayner (New York: Wiley, 1996). Steven Schnaars' *Megamistakes* (New York: The Free Press, 1989) is also entertainingly relevant, especially for over-confident forecasters!

A simple two-page guide can be found at www.contingency-planning-disaster-recovery-guide.co.uk/. There are also some more detailed guidelines and checklists on the UK government site at www.ogc.gov.uk/sdtoolkit/reference/documentation/p37_contingency.html.

Asserting Yourself

Learning areas	**Social skills:** Emotional resilience: Proactivity

Assertiveness is a key skill for managers and leaders. Some of us are naturally assertive; others have to work at it. It is easy to confuse assertiveness with 'pushiness' or aggression. In fact, assertiveness means pursuing your goals *and* the goals of the other people in the situation. It means getting a positive result in unclear or difficult situations where the temptations are to hold back or let things go.

Activity

Step 1

In the following questionnaire, you will find 10 sets of three statements, like this example:

I'm a person who:

(a) has my rights violated
(b) protects my own rights
(c) violates the rights of others.

The scoring is based on the notion that we all behave in each of these ways from time to time, although the extent to which we have a tendency for (a), (b) or (c) will vary.

You are therefore asked to allocate points of each of (a), (b) and (c), such that the total adds up to 10. Thus, if you think that you quite often have your rights violated, and quite often protect the rights of others, but rarely violate the rights of others, you might score yourself as a person who:

(a) has my rights violated | 4
(b) protects my own rights | 4
(c) violates the rights of others | 2
| 10

On the other hand, if you recognize that you protect your own rights at all costs, even if this quite often involves violating the rights of others, then your score might be that you are a person who:

(a) has my rights violated | 0
(b) protects my own rights | 6
(c) violates the rights of others | 4
| 10

Now complete the questionnaire.
I'm a person who:

1. (a) has my rights violated
   (b) protects my own rights
   (c) violates the rights of others
   | 10

2. (a) does not achieve my goals
   (b) achieves my goals without hurting other people
   (c) achieves my goals at the expense of other people
   | 10

3. (a) feels frustrated and unhappy
   (b) feels good about myself
   (c) is defensive and/or belligerent
   | 10

4. (a) is inhibited and withdrawn
   (b) is socially and emotionally expressive
   (c) is explosive, hostile, angry
   | 10

5. (a) feels hurt, anxious
   (b) is quietly self-confident
   (c) is brashly confident, boastful
   | 10

6. (a) fails to achieve my goals
   (b) tries to find ways so that I can achieve my goals *and* others can achieve theirs
   (c) is not concerned about others and their goals

   10

7. (a) is gullible, easily taken in
   (b) is open-minded and questioning
   (c) is suspicious, cynical

   10

8. (a) feels bad about my weaknesses
   (b) is aware of my weaknesses, but don't dislike myself because of them
   (c) is unaware of my weaknesses

   10

9. (a) allows others to choose for me
   (b) chooses for myself
   (c) intrudes on other people's choices

   10

10. (a) is taken advantage of
    (b) protects my own rights
    (c) takes advantage of others

    10

Step 2

This questionnaire is based on a model that suggests that ASSERTION is the 'happy medium' between two equally undesirable extremes – *passivity* and *aggression*.

To see where you are, add up all your (a) scores (*passivity*), (b) scores (*assertion*) and (c) scores (*aggression*), and enter them in Figure A18.1.

This way of looking at assertion is very important. Although it is easy to distinguish assertion from passivity, it is often mistaken and confused with aggression. In fact, however, as the questionnaire statements show, they are very different.

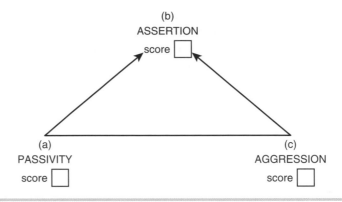

Figure A18.1   Scoring model

Step 3

Make yourself an action plan to build up your assertiveness. You can use Activity 37, *Action planning*, for this. The (b) behaviours tell you what to aim for if you want to become more assertive; these can become the basis of your intentions for actions.

Learning to be assertive takes practice. You have taken the important first step by getting an idea of your passive/assertive/aggressive profile.

Another useful step is to ask other people to fill the questionnaire out on you – what is *their* picture of where you are?

Then ask them:

'In order to become more assertive, what should I …

1.   … do less of?
2.   … do more of?
3.   … start doing?'

Another tip is to keep a diary of how assertive you are at work and outside. You can use Activity 8, *Personal journal*, for this. Record your experiences for two or three weeks, trying to log at least one situation per day. When you have a set of data – analyse it: Do certain situations or people tend to push you into passivity or aggression? What is there about these? What can you do about them?

Other Activities in this book that will help you with ideas about how to build your assertiveness, are those concerned with power, e.g. 9 (*Use your power*), 11 (*Political awareness*), 39 (*Managing upwards*) and 48 (*Managing your dependency*).

Follow-up

There are lots of books on assertiveness. A popular classic is *Assertiveness at Work: A Practical Guide to Handling Awkward Situations*, by Ken Back and Kate Back (Maidenhead: McGraw-Hill, 2005). A simple approach is presented by Max A. Eggert in *The Assertiveness Pocketbook* (Alresford: Management Pocketbooks, 1997), and again by Mary Hartley in *The Assertiveness Handbook* (London: Sheldon Press, 2005)

Assertiveness is one of the topics covered in a wider ranging book, *Influencing Within Organizations*, by Andrzej Huczynski (2nd edition, London: Routledge, 2004). Again broader in scope is the pithy *The Influencing Pocketbook*, by Richard Storey (Alresford: Management Pocketbooks, 2000).

A websearch on assertiveness training produces over 2,000,000 entries. Take your pick!

Handling Conflicts

Handling conflict is an important part of leadership and managerial work. You may need to mediate between conflicting people or be in conflict yourself with someone else competing for the same resources as you. You will certainly be handling crises and unforeseen events.

Conflict situations occur where one party frustrates the goals of other parties and yet they are dependent on each other. The outcomes can vary from outright battling through negotiations and compromise, to walk-overs or avoidance. In particular situations, one response might be more appropriate than another, but no one response is correct every time.

Think about how you respond to conflict. How do you react when faced with frustration and antagonism? The more aware you are of your own personal style, and the bigger your repetoire of responses, the more flexible and successful you will be in resolving particular conflicts.

This activity will help you to look at your usual responses to conflict situations and generate some alternatives for action. It is in three parts: Part 1 contains three case studies to test your responses to particular conflict situations, Part 2 offers a model of conflict resolution styles and Part 3 is a questionnaire to help you determine your preferred approach.

Activity

Part 1: Case studies

For each of the three short cases, write down your first reaction to the situation. Think yourself into the situation and feel the anger, frustration or whatever wells up inside you.

Case 1

You have just arrived at the coffee room and are waiting for your coffee. Across the room you see a colleague with whom you fell out at the last department meeting. The argument concerned the shortage of skilled staff – you believe your department does not get its fair share but that your colleague's is overstaffed. This morning one of your staff failed to report for work and on applying for a pool consultant you were told that the last one had gone to your colleague's department. At the sight of this person, your anger and sense of injustice flood back. What do you do? (Write down your first reaction.)

_____

_____

_____

_____

_____

Case 2

The road on which you live on has a fringe of lawn between the footpath and the road. You look after your section and like to see it looking green and well tended. Most of your neighbours do the same, but on one side of you live some people you don't know too well and who ignore this common policy. They never look after the verge and they and their friends frequently park their cars on it. Recently, they have been parking on your section and, in the recent wet weather, tyre marks have marred the green surface. You have spoken to them once about this, when they appeared off-hand and indifferent to your concern. One Sunday morning you wake at 5 a.m. to an engine noise, and on looking outside see two deep scars across your lawn. At 9 o'clock and still annoyed, you meet your neighbour in the papershop. What do you do? (Write down your first reaction.)

_____

_____

_____

_____

_____

Case 3

You are a young manager in the sales section of a large company. Your boss sends for you one morning and you hear on the grapevine that you will be asked to take on an unpopular duty that involves coming in every other Saturday. You don't like it – you like to keep your weekends free for the family, and you feel you are getting a raw deal because you are junior. You're on your way to the boss's office. What do you do? (Write down your first reaction.)

_____

_____

_____

_____

_____

When you've responded to these three cases, go back over them and see if you can think of *alternative* approaches.

Case 1. Alternative approaches

_____

_____

_____

_____

Case 2. Alternative approaches

_____

_____

_____

_____

_____

Case 3. Alternative approaches

_____

_____

_____

_____

One effect of conflict is that it can lead to stress, rigidity and a hardening of attitudes, which partly explains why we have habitual ways of reacting to conflict situations. Try these questions:

■ Looking back over your initial reactions to the three cases, can you spot a habitual mode of response?

■ Think of conflicts you have had in the past with your spouse, colleagues, parents, etc. Do these show any pattern of response?

■ Of the three cases, how many alternatives to each of your initial responses could you generate? Two? Three? Four? Or more?

The more alternatives you generate, the more chances you have of being flexible in practice.

Part 2: A conflict resolution model

Figure A19.1 shows five conflict-handling styles based on two basic dimensions of conflict situations: in any conflict between two parties the mode of resolution depends upon:

(a) how assertive or unassertive each party is in pursuing its *own goals*
(b) how cooperative or uncooperative each party is in pursuing *the goals of the other*.

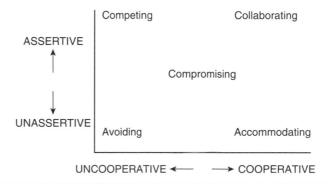

Figure A19.1   Conflict style model

Because conflict resolution is an interactive and reciprocal activity, the style you adopt will affect the style of your partner, and vice versa. If both of you are highly assertive yet uncooperative in terms of each other's goals, then they will adopt a battling, *competing* style; if you are both unassertive of your own goals and also uncooperative, you will tend to avoid the conflict altogether and try to pretend it doesn't exist. And so on.

Use the model in Fig. A19.1 to diagnose a conflict situation in which you have been personally involved (a personal relationship perhaps offers most scope). Can you classify the modes adopted of the two parties and arrive at a description of the joint style of resolution on the chart?

Do this with as many conflict situations as you can think of. By diagnosing your habitual responses in certain situations and observing the responses of others, you can obtain a clearer picture of your own behaviour. Can you answer these questions:

■   When do you avoid conflict?

■   When do you compete with others?

■   Do you ever collaborate in conflict situations?

■   How do you feel when you accommodate to others?

■   How often do you secure compromises?

The more you can identify your own style(s) and the responses generated by others, and the more alternatives you can see in any particular situation, the more likely you are to behave appropriately the next time conflict arises.

Part 3: Conflict management questionnaire

This paired-comparison questionnaire will help you to identify your preferred style of conflict handling.

Choose one of the statements from each of the 30 pairs below. *Choose the one which is most like the way you handle differences between yourself and others:*

1. 1. I am usually firm in pursuing my goals.
    2. I attempt to get all concerns and issues immediately out in the open.
2. 1. I put my cards on the table and invite the other person to do likewise.
    2. When conflicts arise I try to win my case.
3. 1. Once I adopt a position I defend it strongly.
    2. I prefer not to argue but to look for the best solution possible.
4. 1. I sometimes sacrifice my own wishes for the wishes of the other person.
    2. I feel that differences are not always worth worrying about.
5. 1. I accept the views of the other, rather than rock the boat.
    2. I avoid people with strong views.
6. 1. I like to cooperate with others and follow their ideas.
    2. I feel that most things are not worth arguing about. I stick to my own views.
7. 1. I try to find some compromise situation.
    2. I am usually firm in pursuing my goals.
8. 1. When conflicts arise I try to win my case.
    2. I propose a middle ground.
9. 1. I like to meet the other person half-way.
    2. Once I adopt a position I defend it strongly.
10. 1. I feel that differences are not always worth worrying about.
     2. I try to find a compromise solution.
11. 1. I propose a middle ground.
     2. I avoid people with strong views.
12. 1. I feel that most things are not worth arguing about. I stick to my own views.
     2. I like to meet the other person half-way.
13. 1. I am usually firm in pursuing my goals.
     2. I sometimes sacrifice my own wishes for the wishes of the other person.
14. 1. I accept the views of the other, rather than rock the boat.
     2. When conflicts arise I try to win my case.
15. 1. Once I adopt a position I defend it strongly.
     2. I like to cooperate with others and follow their ideas.
16. 1. I try to find a compromise solution.
     2. I sometimes sacrifice my own wishes for the wishes of the other person.
17. 1. I accept the views of the other, rather than rock the boat.
     2. I propose a middle ground.
18. 1. I like to meet the other person half-way.
     2. I like to cooperate with others and follow their ideas.

19. 1. I feel that differences are not always worth worrying about.
    2. I am usually firm in pursuing my goals.
20. 1. When conflicts arise I try to win my case.
    2. I avoid people with strong views.
21. 1. I feel that most things are not worth arguing about. I stick to my own views.
    2. Once I adopt a position I defend it strongly.
22. 1. I attempt to get all concerns and issues immediately out in the open.
    2. I feel that differences are not always worth worrying about.
23. 1. I avoid people with strong views.
    2. I put my cards on the table and invite the other person to do likewise.
24. 1. I prefer not to argue but to look for the best solution possible.
    2. I feel that most things are not worth arguing about. I stick to my own views.
25. 1. I attempt to get all concerns and issues immediately out in the open.
    2. I try to find a compromise solution.
26. 1. I put my cards on the table and invite the other person to do likewise.
    2. I propose a middle ground.
27. 1. I prefer not to argue but to look for the best solution possible.
    2. I like to meet the other person half-way.
28. 1. I sometimes sacrifice my own wishes for the wishes of the other person.
    2. I attempt to get all concerns and issues immediately out in the open.
29. 1. I put my cards on the table and invite the other person to do likewise.
    2. I accept the views of the other, rather than rock the boat.
30. 1. I like to cooperate with others and follow their ideas.
    2. I prefer not to argue but to look for the best solution possible.

Scoring

The key below shows you how to score your questionnaire (Table A19.1).
A, B, C, D and E represent the five conflict handling styles as follows:

A = Avoiding
B = Accommodating
C = Compromising
D = Competing
E = Collaborating.

So, for example, if you chose the second statement of the first pair then you would score 1 for E. If you chose the first statement of the second pair you would score another 1 for E, and so on (see Table A19.1).

The maximum score for any mode is 12 and the total aggregate score is 30. **A score of more than 6 on any mode would indicate a preference for that mode, while a score of less than 6 would indicate relative neglect.**

Table A19.1 Conflict management questionnaire

Statement Pair	Conflict-resolution mode				
	A	B	C	D	E
1				1	2
2				2	1
3				1	2
4	2	1			
5	2	1			
6	2	1			
7			1	2	
8			2	1	
9			1	2	
10	1		2		
11	2		1		
12	1		2		
13		2		1	
14		1		2	
15		2		1	
16		2	1		
17		1	2		
18		2	1		
19	1			2	
20	2			1	
21	1			2	
22	2				1
23	1				2
24	2				1
25			2		1
26			2		1
27			2		1
28		1			2
29		2			1
30		1			2
Total					

What do these results mean to you?

- Do you have some dominant ways of approaching conflicts?
- Are there styles that you do not make use of?
- What would you like to change?

The questionnaire is a one-point-in-time measure of your reaction to conflict situations. It has validity in so far it corroborates with your own perception of your preferred style and the results you got from the cases earlier in this exercise If these point in the same direction, then a conclusion is comparatively simple. More uneven results will require puzzling out. Other people's opinions will be especially useful here – particularly those with whom you have had your differences!

Follow-up

You need practice and application to develop further your skills in resolving conflicts. Activity 18 *Asserting yourself,* is very relevant here because the ideas have a direct bearing on how you orient yourself to conflict situations. Activity 8, *Personal journal,* could be used to help you learn from your own conflict experiences.

One of the best and most straightforward books on negotiating and managing conflict is Fisher, Ury and Patton's *Getting to Yes* (revised edition, New York: Random House, 2003). The ubiquitous Management Pocketbooks have a good little guide *The Resolving Conflict Pocketbook* by Max Eggert (2003). A deeper treatment but still filled with practical insights is Friedrich Glasl's *Confronting Conflict: A First-aid Kit for handling Conflict* (Stroud: Hawthorn Press, 1999). More interpersonal approaches can be found in *Managing Conflict Through Communication*, by Dudley Cahn and Roxane Lulofs (Boston: Allyn and Bacon, 2006) and Myra Isenhart and Michael Spangle's *Collaborative Approaches to Resolving* Conflict (Thousand Oaks: Sage, 2000).

Conflict is another popular topic on the world-wide web with over 37,000,000 references on Google.

Getting the Best Out of Groups

Social Skills: Sensitivity to events:
Analytical skills: Proactivity

How much of your time at work is spent in groups? Partnerships, project teams, committees, consortia and other meetings may account for over half of your time at work. The trend towards partnerships and shared leadership adds to this load.

Groups are used for many vital functions, especially in information sharing and making sense, reaching consensus and making decisions. All of these processes can be difficult and energy-consuming. Every leader and manager needs to learn about how to get the best out of groups and how to make teams as effective as they can be.

The aim of this activity is to improve your understanding and skill in handling behaviour in groups. It does this by offering a process for observing behaviours in groups and also by inviting you to experiment with your own group behaviours.

Activity

Part 1: Measuring the contribution rate

A first exercise in group observation and analysis is to take a 'contribution count'. At your next meeting, choose a 10- or 15-minute period, when you can concentrate on observing rather than contributing.

Write the name or identifying mark for each member of the group on a sheet of paper. Over 10 or 15 minutes, note each contribution made by each group member by putting a mark beside their names. See Fig. A20.1, where the 'five-barred gate method' is used.

A 'contribution' is any spoken comment to the group (not an aside to another member) although it may be directed at one person in particular.

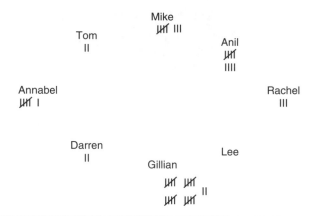

Figure A20.1   Contribution roles in a group

It may be short or long, although you could put two marks for a contribution of more than, say, 30 seconds.

Figure A20.1 shows clear differences between the group members in terms of the number of contributions made:

Gillian 22
Anil 9 } HIGH contributors

Mike 8
Annabel 6 } MEDIUM contributors

Rachel 3
Tom 2
Darren 2
Lee 0 } LOW contributors

Now, why did Gillian and Anil contribute most? Because they have the most to say, or because they are the more senior? In either case, does their dominance help or hinder the group in its task? If they knew most about the subject under discussion, or because they were the two principal speakers for and against an idea, then this might well help the group achieve its goals.

What about Rachel, Tom, Darren, and Lee? Did they just have nothing to contribute, or were they shut out, asleep, junior or 'unlistened-to' members?

Share your contribution count with the other members of your group – although you will need a good relationship or, better still, a contract with them to do this. If the group takes notice of the observation, it can provoke useful changes.

A contribution count can tell you a lot about a group, especially over a number of meetings. Behaviour patterns form quickly and we tend to conform to these – although this is done at a subconscious level of which we are not fully aware unless it is brought to our attention. Equally, a contribution count measures only a fraction of what goes on in a group situation, and it should not be taken for more than it is. It takes no account of the *quality* of the contribution; of non-verbal behaviour, of the requirements of the particular situation or of how people are feeling.

However, it has the great advantage of being easy to do. For a more advanced version of 'the contribution count', in your next meeting, observe as before but now log in addition:

- Who talks to whom. Who do they direct their remarks at and look at when they speak?
- Who interrupts whom?
- Who finally makes the decision – one person, two persons, the whole group?

These are the more difficult to measure, but will give you useful data for your own reflection and, if you can introduce it, for the greater effectiveness of the group.

Part 2: Categorizing behaviour in groups

The effectiveness of groups depends largely upon right behaviour at the right time. The group behaviour categories shown in Table A20.1 were developed and pioneered by Neil Rackham and have been used to improve group effectiveness at British Airways and many other organizations.

Here are just eight categories for you to practise with. Again, chose a 10–15-minute session to observe. Use an observation sheet with categories down the left-hand side and group members' names along the top as in Table A20.2.

Practise on two or four behaviours and two or four people until you get the hang of it. Try logging Gillian and Anil on 'proposing', 'giving information' 'seeking information' and 'supporting/building'. High contributors often do a lot of proposing and giving information but less information seeking.

Some groups do a lot of giving information and making proposals, but do very little seeking information or understanding. Building and summarizing tend to be a rare behaviours. 'Defending/attacking' creates similar responses in others, and a sort of escalation or spiral occurs.

From your observations over a number of meetings and 15-minute periods you should be able to answer some of the following:

- Do people fall into habitual roles? Are there habitual low contributors or chronic proposers or consenters who do no disagreeing?
- Is there a balance of behaviour in the group? People may fall into particular roles, but if these complement each other then the group may

Table A20.1 Categories of group behaviour

Category	Definition
Proposing	– a behaviour which puts forward a new concept, suggestion or course of action: 'I suggest we call a meeting of all Department employees'
Giving information	– a behaviour which offers facts, opinions or clarification to others: 'There is a full definition of this in the handbook'
Seeking information	– a behaviour which seeks facts, opinions or clarification from others: 'What do the rest of you think?'
Supporting/building	– a behaviour which declares support or agreement with another person or attempts to extend or develop a proposal made by another person: 'I agree with Lee and moreover we should start now'
Disagreeing	– a behaviour which involves a direct criticism, difference of opinion or disagreement with another person's idea: 'No my boss would never accept a reduction in his budget'
Defending/attacking	– a behaviour which attacks another person or defends an individual's own position. More emotional than disagreeing: 'That is a stupid idea' or 'My idea is better than that'
Blocking/difficulty stating	– a behaviour which blocks another proposal without offering alternatives and without reasons: 'It won't work' or 'We can't have that'
Testing understanding	– a behaviour which checks and seeks to establish whether an earlier contribution has been understood: 'Can I just ask you, Anil, did you imply that you were supporting or not supporting Mike's proposal?
Summarizing	– a behaviour which summarizes, or restates concisely, the content of a previous proposal or discussion: 'Well, so far, ladies and gentlemen, we have heard two proposals: Tom's – to call a meeting immediately; and Anil's – to delay action until next week'

function well. But unless somebody *is* doing the summarizing, testing understanding, supporting, etc., several vital functions will be missing.

■ How could this group work better? For example, does everybody feel OK about their roles, levels of contribution and rewards from this group? Does the group make good decisions without undue wasting of time?

Table A20.2 Observation sheet for of group behaviour

Observation sheet		Date						Time	
Names	Anil	Gillian	Mike	Tom	Annabel	Lee	Rachel	Darren	Total
Proposing	II	⟊⟊ I	⟊⟊		I		I	I	16
Giving information	I	IIII	⟊⟊ III	I	II	II	I	I	20
Seeking information	III	I	⟊⟊ I	III					

. . . and so on . . .

Good groups will welcome your observations, but many groups are unused to self-scrutiny and may be defensive. Caution is recommended.

Part 3

You can dispense with the caution and be as experimental as you like with your own behaviour. After your observations you will have some ideas about the way you behave in groups. Spend some time now summarizing these.

Step 1: What characteristics have you noticed in yourself?

- Are you a medium, low, or high contributor?

- Are you a proposer, a builder, or what?

- How much seeking behaviour do you practise?

- What happened the last time you were in a defending/attacking position?

- How often do you test your understanding of other people's ideas?

Step 2: Now do some experimenting. Choose some of the behaviours that you would like to do more of, and some you'd like to cut back on and follow the steps below:

2.1. At the next meeting you attend, experiment by using one new behaviour. If you're trying to lessen a behaviour, try cutting it out altogether.
What is this behaviour?
2.2. Carefully observe what effect you're having. You may be able to get feedback how people react to you in the meeting or by conversations afterwards.
2.3. If you're stuck for behaviours to try, remember that seeking information, building, summarizing, and testing understanding are often low in groups.

Here are some suggested actions. At the next meeting try one of the following:

- Do nothing but ask questions.
- Never ask a question.
- Do not agree or disagree with anything.
- Each time you're not absolutely sure what another person means, ask for clarification.
- If you're normally a high contributor – say nothing; if you're normally low – aim to say more than anyone else.

Follow-up

This type of analysis was first undertaken by Robert Bales and his colleagues more than 50 years ago. David Buchanan and Andrej Huczynski's massive (nearly 1000 pages) *Organisational Behaviour: An Introductory Text* (5th edition, London: Financial Times Prentice-Hall, 2004) devotes a major part to behaviour in groups.

Many people find the neuro-liguistic programming approach to inter-personal behaviour useful; one text here is Sue Knights' *NLP at Work: The Difference that Makes a Difference in Business* (London: Nicholas Brealey, 2002). Finally, Mike Pedler and Tom Boydell's *Managing Yourself* (3rd edition, London: Lemos and Crane, 1999) has a chapter focused on working with other people.

What Are You Like?

Learning areas	**Social skills:** Self-knowledge: Analytical skills

Your success and failure in achieving things with and through people depend a lot on how you see and make judgements about other people and you see yourself in relation to them.

Any action you take to influence another person is based on a complex set of assumptions about how they will interpret your action and the way in which they will respond to it.

Part 1 of this activity is designed to help you become aware of the ways in which you see other people and yourself. Part 2 suggests that you check this out to see how your perceptions coincide with those of others.

Activity

Part 1

Step 1

In Column 1 of Fig. A21.1, write the names of five people with whom you interact frequently at work.

Columns 2 and 3 of Fig. A21.1 each have ten boxes, joined in pairs by horizontal lines. The lines represent dimensions of difference between people; for example: kind – aloof; aggressive – meek, clever – stupid; honest – devious, and so on.

Take each dimension in turn and look at the names of the people in the two boxes joined to it by the lines between Columns 1 and 2. Think of a way in which these two people seem different to you in some way, and a pair of words

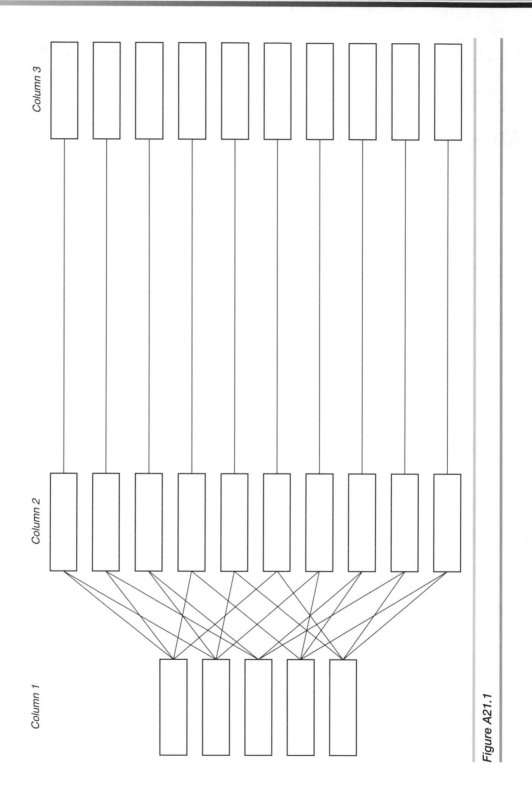

Figure A21.1

such as the ones exampled above which describes the difference you perceive between them.

Put one word in the box at each end of the dimension (it doesn't matter which word goes at which end). Do this for each of the ten dimensions, using a different dimension (and therefore pair of words) each time. As this is a short activity, don't worry that you haven't covered all the differences between people; the idea is to get a sense of the ways in which you classify people.

Step 2

Now, treating each of the ten dimensions as a scale, put a cross to show where you think you are as a person, and mark it with your initials (see Fig. A21.2).

Figure A21.2

Think of each scale as running from extreme to extreme, e.g. very reliable to very unreliable, even if the people from whom you derived this dimension in the first place are not at the extremes.

Now think about yourself and your close working colleagues. How do you see yourself in relation to them?

The dimensions that you have chosen are ways in which you distinguish between people – therefore, they are likely to be important qualities or characteristics in your eyes.

Does this give you a sense of how you make judgements about people and on what grounds?

Part 2

If Part 1 gave you useful food for thought about yourself in relation to your colleagues, you can take this activity further with some of the following possibilities:

(a) Decide what you would like to be like by ticking the dimensions where you would like to be.
(b) Try *being* different. If you can do so, is it what you really want?

(c) Choose one of your five colleagues; mark where you think they are on each dimension and then show it to him or her. How do they see themselves compared with yourself?

(d) Repeat (c) with other colleagues.

The key to understanding how you see yourself and others is to develop the habit of checking your perceptions with the other people with whom you work.

Follow-up

This activity is based on George Kelly's Personal Construct Psychology and his notion of the Repertory Grid. See Activity 12, *Credulous listening*, for some follow-up references.

Getting to Know You

Learning areas	**Social skills:** Self-knowledge

To know someone well, we need to get beyond the trivial. Getting to know someone involves learning more about them, their ideas, hopes, fears and ambitions. For the other person to reveal these things about themselves, it is likely that at we will have to reveal significant aspects of ourselves and of our lives in turn. This mutual exchange of personal information can lead to a better understanding and acceptance of each other.

However, our natural reticence and everyday social norms usually stop us talking so openly even with fairly close acquaintances. This activity can be used in any situation where you want to get to know somebody else reasonably well, reasonably quickly. At the same time, you'll find that sharing this personal information will increase your own self-understanding.

Activity

Before you undertake this activity with anyone, make sure that each of you *wants* to get to know the other better. You can't do this unless you are both 'up for it'.

Find a place where you won't be disturbed and set aside at least an hour.

Instructions

Read these instructions carefully before looking at Table A22.1.

Table A22.1 consist of a set of incomplete statement. Start with the first one, and take it in turn to complete the statement, telling the other person as much or as little as you want. *NB. It is entirely up to each person to decide how much or how little to say.* Your partner can respond to what you say in any way they like. Then the other person completes the statement as above. When you have both said enough, move on to statement 2, and so on.

Don't look ahead at the other statements – concentrate only on the one being discussed.

Stop this activity whenever either of you wishes to do so.

Table A22.1   The statements

1. My name is...
2. My job is...
3. My age is...
4. I live...
5. I was born in...
6. My previous jobs included...
7. Things I like best about this job are...
8. Things I like least about this job are...
9. To me, being a woman/man...
10. My marital status is...
11. Children...
12. My parents...
13. My friends...
14. My hobbies/spare-time activities...
15. When I get to work...
16. When I leave work...
17. At this very minute, I feel...
18. Ideally, this time next year...
19. In the long term, my ambition...
20. The trouble with this organization is...
21. My idea of an ideal holiday would be...
22. Things that I find very difficult...
23. If the worst comes to the worst in 12 months' time...
24. The sort of things I worry about...
25. What this country needs...
26. My religious beliefs...
27. To me, being black/white...
28. My secret fears...
29. My feelings about you...
30. My feelings about myself are...

Follow-up

When you have finished this activity:

■ What did you learn about yourself and the other person?

_____

_____

_____

_____

_____

■ Do you think that it has improved your relationship?

_____

_____

_____

_____

_____

Getting to Yes

Learning areas	**Social skills:** Emotional resilience: Sensitivity to events

"Getting to Yes *[by Fisher and Ury] is by far the best thing I've ever read about negotiation*"

J. K. Galbraith

Step 1

Consider the following statements and decide which list – A or B – best describes how you are likely to behave in a negotiation:

A	B
Yield to pressure	Pile on pressure
Make offers	Make threats
Trust others	Distrust others
Search for the single answer, the one they will accept	Hold out for the single answer, the one you will accept

Which is most like you – A or B?

Activity 18, *Asserting yourself*, looks at how we behave with others – passively, aggressively or assertively. Simply put, passive behaviour allows others to walk over us, aggressive behaviour means we walk over others (and their rights), whereas assertive behaviour allows each of us to walk forward.

Applying this to negotiation, the soft negotiator wants to avoid conflict, and so readily makes concessions to reach agreement. However, as in a personal relationship, they may end up feeling exploited. The hard negotiator sees the situation as a contest of wills, in which those who shout loudest and hold out longest fare best. Such archetypal aggressive behaviour may yield short-term gains, but over time is likely to damage relationships, and eventually isolate the aggressor.

A third way is both hard and soft, and assumes that you can obtain what you are entitled to and still behave decently. Here negotiation is approached and seen as a 'making' process, where the parties build and make an agreement with which all can live.

Step 2

The *principled negotiation* approach was developed at the Harvard Negotiation Project and is designed to produce agreements which are both fair and fully implementable. There are four principles:

1. *Separate the people from the problem*
   Go easy on the people but hard on the problem
2. *Focus on interests, not positions*
   Explore mutual interests, rather than make offers or issue threats.
3. *Invent options for mutual gain*
   Designing good solutions under pressure is difficult. Adversarial situations tend to narrow vision and imagination. One way round this is to set aside an agreed period of time in which to develop a wide range of possible solutions that advance *shared interests*.
4. *Insist on objective criteria*
   An aggressive negotiator may try to get their way through intransigence. The assertive negotiator can insist that fair standards, e.g. market value, independent expert advice, health and safety regulations, is used.

Step 3

Think of a current or forthcoming negotiation. This might be at work: over-scarce resources, a joint project, etc.; or at home: over holidays, childcare and so on. Choose a situation where the parties have roughly equal power (because dealings between people with very unequal power has a different flavour).

Thinking of your negotiation, use the four principles to analyse it as in Table A23.1. Jot down ideas for applying principled negotiation to your situation. A supportive friend will be helpful here.

Step 4

Preparation is always vital in negotiation. Make the time to develop your ideas before you meet the other party. If you are part of a team, set aside time to brainstorm the options for mutual gain.

Table A23.1   Four principles of negotiation

1 Separate the people from the problem	2 Focus on interests not positions	3 Invent options for mutual gain	4 Insist on objective criteria

This is good preparation in more than one sense, for it will often develop a sense of unity in a team. However, remember that you are inventing possibilities and options prior to working with the other party and not trying to reach firm decisions and make your mind up yet – stay loose.

Follow-up

This activity is based on one of the best and most straightforward books on negotiating and managing conflict – Fisher, Ury and Patton's *Getting to Yes* (revised edition, New York: Random House, 2003). Roger Fisher has written many other books in this field, including, with co-author Daniel Shapiro, *Beyond Reason: Using Emotions as You Negotiate* (New York: Random House, 2006). He also provides the foreword in the broader *Difficult Conversations: How to Discuss What Matters Most*, by Douglas Stone, Bruce Patton and Sheila Heen (New York: Penguin, 2000). Management Pocketbooks have a short guide – *The Negotiator's Pocketbook* by Patrick Forsyth (2000).

Collaborative Working

Learning areas	**Social Skills:** Emotional resilience: Creativity

Task forces, teams and partnerships have assumed greater importance with the increase in strategic alliances, joint ventures, collaborative projects and inter-agency working. All these joint efforts involve pooling resources, concentrating expertise and bringing together energy and effort across departmental and organizational boundaries. However, all projects have their difficulties, and, as much of the effort always seems to go into the technical side, they often crop up on the social, interpersonal and political side.

Projects put a premium on collaborative work. Working with people with whom we have no formal responsibility or authority often leads to conflicts of loyalty where departments and project teams pull in different directions. Lack of clarity as to what to expect of each other can cause tension and frustration. Resentments, lack of cooperation and incomplete development of the project may appear if the practical issues of working together are not discussed and resolved. For collaborations to be effective, good 'rules of engagement' need to be established.

The following activity will help you prepare for collaborative working. Work through it by relating it to a specific project in which you are about to be involved.

Activity

Step 1

List all the things that you would be prepared to *share* in a collaborative working relationship. Here is the start a possible list – to which you can add:

1. office space

2. administrative back-up

3. access to your equipment

4. your client files

5. your best ideas

6. your mobile phone

7. your favourite lunch venue

8. other resources

9. ? etc.

You could add certain provisos – 'will share office space as long as it's left tidy'.

Now make a list of the things your would *not* be willing to share – you might want to swap things from this list to your 'share' list, and again to add items not mentioned:

1. your professional networks and contacts

2. your books

3. your departmental budget

4. your time outside work

5. ? etc.

Step 2

When you have made your lists, ask yourself: *What are my worries about this project?*

Note these carefully, e.g. consequences of failure?, extra workload?, concerns about particular team members?, worries about disclosing know-how or information?, etc.

Step 3

Any collaborative project is a powerful learning opportunity. What learning goals could you accomplish via this project? Here are a few possible examples to start you off:

- ■ to widen my knowledge outside my professional field
- ■ to increase my visibility with senior people
- ■ to gain experience of other parts of the company/industry
- ■ to put myself into a high-risk situation
- ■ to improve my group working and management skills and so on.

Now think about what you could *offer* to your partners: what knowledge, skills or personal qualities are you prepared to offer to other people on this project, what:

- knowledge?
- skills?
- personal qualities?

Step 4

Next think about the qualities you would like in project colleagues. Complete the following sentences:

What I want are people who *know*_____

_____

What I want are people who *can*_____

_____

What I want are people who *will*_____

_____

You could include standards of behaviour in this list. How should this person behave towards your staff, your boss, yourself? What actions will provoke resentment (e.g. borrowing things without asking, not listening to suggestions, using offensive language)?

While you are at it, is there any way you might need to moderate or change you own behaviour?

Step 5

Next, draft some ground rules in plain terms covering how you and the others can work together. These can cover any of the issues you have covered above, e.g.

Sample ground rules

- Work from a basic assumption of equality – in terms of ideas, rights, etc.
- Make time to listen to each other's ideas.
- Willingness to share resources in terms of administration, files, work space, etc.

- No smoking in work areas.
- Build in time for 'after action reviews' for learning purposes.
- Agree to refer disputes to an external facilitator/arbitrator.
- Etc.

Step 6

Finally, agree a joint set of Ground Rules at an early meeting with the whole project team. Keep this agreed list – perhaps pinned to the wall as a guide to good behaviour. From time to time you can review the Ground Rules together – do they need revising? Do we need to add anything?

Follow-up

There are many books on partnership working. *The Partnering Imperative*, by Anne Deering and Anne Murphy (Chichester: Wiley, 2003), is based on research into partnerships and John Carlisle and Robert Parker's *Beyond Negotiation* (Chichester: Wiley, 1989) is also good. Other useful books include John Child and David Faulkner's *Strategies of Co-operation: Managing Alliances, Networks and Joint Ventures* (Oxford: Oxford University Press, 1998), *The Strategic Partnering Handbook*, by Tony Lendrum (Roseville, NSW: McGraw-Hill, 2000) and *Business Partnering for Continuous Improvement: How to Forge Enduring Alliances Among Employees, Suppliers and Customers*, by Charles Poirier and William Hoser (San Francisco: Berrett-Koehler, 1994).

The not-for-profit Partnering Initiative, http://thepartneringinitiative.org/mainpages/about/intro/, produces a number of very useful tools and other resources, most of which are free of charge.

Be a Coach!

Learning areas	**Social skills:** Professional knowledge: Balanced learning habits

It is said that every *good* manager and leader is a coach. Think of the best manager you have ever had: did they make time to coach you?

In addition to helping other people, being a coach is also one of the best ways of learning for yourself: 'See one, do one, teach one', as the old surgeon's motto has it.

Questioning is at the heart of good coaching. This Activity is based on the GROW model, which is perhaps the most widespread model used in this work. It is a framework and a checklist of the sorts of questions that a coach can use in coaching both individuals and teams. You can be a coach. You should be a coach for others and for yourself.

Activity

The questions offered in this Activity can be used to start the coaching session, during the session to draw out the learning, clarify expectations and set goals, or after to summarize and review the learning.

Step 1

Find a friend or colleague who is prepared to be coached by you. This can be someone new to the organization or someone who is facing a tricky situation that they would like to think through.

Be open with this person about your own coaching skills. If this is new for you, then explain that you want to develop your skills in this area and learn about the coaching process. Explain how you are intending to go about it. Agree in advance that you will have a joint review session where you can get feedback from your partner on how helpful they found the process and how you could improve.

Step 2

Once you have a partner to be coached, agree a contract for three coaching sessions at regular intervals – weekly or monthly, for example.

Set times for these sessions and put them in your diaries. Allow an hour for each session.

Step 3

The coaching process is one of guided questioning to help the person move forward with their issue or situation. In your first session, follow the sequence of the GROW Model (Fig. A25.1) in seeking to guide your partner through an exploration of the goal that they are trying to achieve, an evaluation of the options for action and a testing of their commitment to achieve the goal:

G GOAL – *Setting goals for the task in general, or for this session.*
R REALITY – *Testing and raising awareness of the current situation.*
O OPTIONS – *Finding alternative strategies, solutions, answers and ways forward.*
W WILL – *Testing commitment to goals, & making concrete, realistic plans and steps to reach them.*

Complete the first coaching session in 50 minutes and keep the last 10 minutes for reviewing the effectiveness of the session with your partner.

Step 4

How did you do? What did you learn from the first coaching session?

If you ran out of questions or ideas, some further questions to help with each of the stages of the GROW model, are given in Fig. A25.2.

These questions are offered as a guide – nothing more. Use any that fit your natural style and language and do not slavishly follow the G–R–O–W sequence if it is not working.

If it seems to you that there is a better question arising from the situation or if it seems better to start with first steps and work backwards, try that out – whatever works for you and the other person.

The GROW Model: *Goal, Reality, Options, Will*

GOAL

- What is it you want to achieve?
- When you get there, what will it look like, sound like, and feel like?
- When you achieve this, what else will it help you to do?

REALITY

- What is happening at the moment?
- What are you dissatisfied about?
- What else is happening at the moment?
- Who is involved in the situation and what are they doing?
- What do you want to take forward from what is happening at present?

OPTIONS

- What options for action do you have?
- What else have you though of (and rejected)?
- Have you thought of...?
- Do you have the resources to make the change?
- Who could help you in this?

WILL

- Which option do you most favour?
- How committed are you to taking this action (on a scale of 1–10)?
- What do you need to do to increase your will to do this?
- What support do you need?
- What is the first step you will take?
- When?

Figure A25.1   GROW model

GOAL

- What exactly do you want to achieve – short and long term?
- How will you know if you reach your goal?
- Is any part of it measurable?
- Why is the goal desirable, challenging and achievable for you?
- How would you rate your achievements so far, in this respect?
- How can you break down the goal into more manageable sub-goals?

REALITY

- Why haven't you reached this goal already?
- What have you done so far?
- What have you learnt from that?
- Who will there be the winners and losers if you get what you want?
- What is *really* stopping you?
- What constraints – *inside and outside yourself* – are holding you back?
- How might you overcome these?
- How might you sabotage your own efforts?

OPTIONS

- What else could you do? (Repeat this question until you both get fed up with it)
- What would you do if time and resources were not an issue?
- How could you change yourself so that is would not be a problem?
- What would happen if you did nothing?
- Whom do you admire or respect who does this really well?
- What might this person do in your situation?

WILL

- How does this goal fit in with your other personal priorities?
- Which option(s) will you choose?
- How will that help you?
- What could possibly go wrong? (How will you overcome them?)
- Who else should know about your plan? (How will you inform them?)
- How committed are you really to this?
- If your commitment is low, might it be better to find something that you *really* want to do?
- What is Plan B?

Figure A25.2   Further GROW questions

Most of all coaching is a relationship and if the other person wants sympathy or clear direction, information or feedback, then go with that – as long as you feel it is appropriate.

Follow-up

Coaching has always been one of the most useful approaches to one-to-one management development and there are many books and websites available, many of them utilizing the GROW model or something similar.

One of the best-known books in this field is John Whitmore's *Coaching for Performance: Growing People, Performance and Purpose* (London: Nicholas Brealey, 2002). Also try David Clutterbuck and David Megginson's *Techniques for Coaching and Mentoring* (Oxford: Butterworth-Heinemann, 2005).

These last authors are involved in the European Mentoring and Coaching Council (EMCC), which brings together practitioners, researchers and institutions and is attempting to regulate this new profession: www.emccouncil.org.

Finally, a book with a broader and somewhat different focus but which may also be helpful is Roger Schwartz's *The Skilled Facilitator: A Comprehensive Resource for Consultants, Facilitators, Managers, Trainers and Coaches* (New York: Jossey Bass Wiley, 2003). This is almost all it claims to be.

Difficult Situations

We all face 'difficult situations' from time to time, both in our work and in our personal lives. We define a difficult situation as one in which (i) something very important is at stake or (ii) things are not going right or there seems to be no obvious way forward: situations in which you feel 'in a corner', 'between a rock and a hard place', or 'on a burning platform'.

For example, it may be a target that you can see no way of meeting, but one that you will be punished for if you fail. Or, you may find yourself falling out with someone you want to get on well with, or find that an esteemed colleague that you do not want to offend is doing something of which you deeply disapprove. And so on; there are lots of difficult situations.

How do you cope in situations like this?

It may or may not be a comfort to remember that in seemly impossible situations that nothing stays the same for ever, that there is a future, that something else will happen. The thing to worry about is how to cope and how to shape this new situation. As Friedrich Nietzsche said, "that which does not kill me makes me strong" – emotional resilience is built by learning to cope with adversity.

Five options for difficult situations

There are five ways out of a difficult situation: love it, leave it, live with it, change it or change yourself.

■ *Love it* – this means asking yourself why you are so concerned about the difficult situation – what makes you stick in there and try to deal with it – if we really think about it we may find some core of ourselves that finds it worthwhile to struggle with this one – the struggle is the measure of our caring. It may also be possible (probably sometimes not always) to 'reframe' the situation into a more positive light – the breaking down of something may give the opportunity to re-build it in a more positive way.

■ *Leave it* – on the other hand, do you want to stick in there with it? Why not just walk away? Does it have to be your problem? What exactly are the costs of getting out of it? Might they be less than the costs of staying in with it? Are there some benefits to walking away from it? A more constructive use of your energies?

■ *Live with it* – which is what we are doing while we work out what to do. Can you just go on like this? What actually happens if you do nothing? What is the worst that can happen? Are there any defensive moves you can make to lessen the pain while leaving it alone? Things and situations do change – if you do nothing, it is possible that things will right themselves of their own accord, even if it seems difficult to imagine how they might do so now. Sometimes anything you might do has a greater chance of making things worse rather than better, so why not leave it alone?

■ *Change it* – let's look at it one more time – what would it actually take to deal with the situation? If you had a magic wand, what would you do? Is it that other people do not see that there is a problem, or see it the same way we do? What would it take to tell them and ask them to help us change it? Do you need to be more assertive in this situation? Are you being creative enough in your search for solutions? What would the most effective and successful person you know do with this situation?

■ *Change yourself* – Is the situation difficult because you are hanging on to some idea of yourself – as competent, respected, popular or something else? These things may be very special for us and non-negotiable, but maybe not. Can you make the difficulty reduce or go away by changing our idea of who you are or who you want to be?

Activity

Use this framework to think about difficult situations in you life – past, present and future. This activity is simply a thought experiment – applying these ideas to difficult situations that you have, and might face in the future.

Past

Think of the most difficult situation that you have faced in the past:

■ Which of the five avenues did you take or try?
■ What worked?

- What did not work for you?
- Which did you try first and which did you try later?
- How did you resolve it in the end?

Present

What is the most difficult situation facing you now? Think about what each of the options looks like for this.

- Which do you rule out and why?
- Which is the best or least bad of them?
- What can you do to make it more acceptable?

Future

Is there a particular difficult situation coming your way?

If not, what general kinds of difficulty do you think might come up for you in the future? Can you think of ways of setting things up so that at least one of the five options will work for you?

Conclusion

Looking back over this Activity – do you have a general habit or pattern in how you deal with difficult situations?

For example, are you always trying to change other people when it may not be realistic? Or, are you always trying to escape from difficulties? Does this get you into trouble? Should you try to broaden your repertoire of coping approaches?

Follow-up

A little philosophy may help in such difficult situations. Try the master in a well-translated version: Friedrich Nietzsche's *Why I am So Wise* is translated by R. J. Hollingdale (London: Penguin, 2004).

Are You Stressed?

Learning areas	**Emotional resilience:** Self-knowledge

Stress-related diseases are a major killer of leaders, managers and professional workers. More than a century ago we learned that the inhalation of dust and fumes led to lung disease and silicosis. We are now learning what causes coronary heart disease, cancer and strokes, and it is increasingly obvious that these diseases are related to the way we live and work. This includes what we eat, how much we exercise, how much tension and pressure we experience and how we handle them.

Looking after ourselves is not just about avoiding an early grave, because the killers (heart disease and cancer) head an unpleasant list of usually non-fatal ailments, including arthritis, asthma, chronic anxiety, colitis, diabetes, eczema, hypertension, mental illness, neurosis, migraines and many other symptoms of physical, emotional and mental distress.

How are you feeling so far? This is not a pretty picture and it's not surprising that many of us close our eyes to it. This activity starts with a short questionnaire on how you behave at work.

Activity

Step 1: Work habits questionnaire

How are you at work? Relaxed, tolerant and easy-going? Or are you tense, easily frustrated and irritable?

Circle the number on each scale in Table A27.1 that best characterizes your *usual* response or behaviour at work, i.e. 1 or 5 if you are *very* like the behaviour described at that end; 2 or 4 if you lean towards that end; and 3 if you genuinely feel in the middle.

Table A27.1 Work habits questionnaire

uncompetitive, avoid conflict	1 2 3 4 5	highly competitive, I like battles
do things at an easy pace	1 2 3 4 5	do things quickly, (walk, eat, drive, etc.)
feel as though there's always plenty of time	1 2 3 4 5	feel as though there's never enough time
have many hobbies and interests	1 2 3 4 5	am only interested in work, I talk a lot about work
always do one thing at a time	1 2 3 4 5	usually keep several balls in the air at once
never hurry	1 2 3 4 5	am always rushing about, always in a hurry
take time off to relax and to think things over	1 2 3 4 5	feel guilty about taking time off to relax
am casual about timekeeping	1 2 3 4 5	am never late

TOTAL SCORE ... _____ (sum of all the ringed numbers)

Step 2

This questionnaire is based on the work of two cardiologists, Friedman and Rosenman (1974), who have suggested that certain types of behaviour are much more likely to lead to coronary heart disease. A composite of these gives us the 'Type A' person, who is:

■ very competitive
■ continually striving for achievement
■ forever in a hurry
■ liable to explosive outbursts of 'free floating aggression'
■ tense, pressurized, urgent, 'hyped up'.

By contrast, the 'Type B' person is:

■ relaxed
■ able to play without guilt
■ able to become absorbed in books, entertainments, conversations and other non-work interests

■   not easily irritated, frustrated or angered
■   in little need of displaying achievements.

Step 3: Scoring

If you scored between:

■   8 and 15 then you're a definite 'Type B' person
■   16 and 23 then you lean towards the 'Type B' person
■   exactly 24 then you're well balanced between the two
■   25 and 32 then you lean towards 'Type A'
■   33 and 40 they you're definitely 'Type A'.

An absolute 'Type B' person would be so 'laid back' that leading and managing activities would either be impossible or not worth the trouble! The important point is that much of this sort of work reinforces any natural tendencies we have and actually *requires* 'Type A' behaviours. We are rewarded for displaying them. This is the main way in which such work forms us – or rather, deforms us.

Follow-up

To start treating yourself better, see the next Activity, *Treat yourself well.*

There are many books around on managing stress. To start with you might go to the ubiquitous Management Pocketbook series with Mary Richards' *The Stress Pocketbook* (Alresford: Management Pocketbooks, 1999). A current best-seller is *The Worry Cure: Stop Worrying and Start Living*, by Robert Leahy (London: Piatkus, 2006).

The *Relaxation and Stress Reduction Workbook* by Martha Davis, Elizabeth Robbins and Matthew Mckay (Oakland, CA: New Harbinger Publications, 2000) is more wide-ranging. A very different approach – deeper and more thoughtful about many issues that underlie feelings of stress, is Angus Jenkinson's *From Stress to Serenity* (Forest Row, Sussex: Sophia Books, 2003). Finally, *Managing Workplace Stress: A Best Practice Blueprint*, by Stephen Williams and Lesley Cooper (Chichester: Wiley, 2002) focuses not on your own personal stress management but on the organizational strategies and managerial actions required for reducing stress.

Treat Yourself Well

Learning areas	**Emotional resilience:** Self-knowledge

"Leaders get attacked, dismissed, silenced and sometimes assassinated because they come to represent loss"

Ronald Heifetz

Leadership work can be dangerous and stressful. There are those times when you are *the* person, the woman or man in charge and you have to take the brunt of the blame or criticism or general 'flak' – often on behalf of others or for the organization as a whole. This is part of the territory.

As we saw in Activity 27, this can lead to a highly stressed lifestyle, which can kill or disable you if you do not take care of yourself.

Activity

Some of the best ways of avoiding the worst effects of leadership and managerial work are to do with building up your inner strength with healthy habits.

Step 1: Healthy habits

Tick any of these that you do habitually and add any of your own to the end.

1. I build up resistance by regular sleep, a healthy diet and plenty of exercise.
2. I talk problems through with my partner.

3. I talk problems through with my boss or colleagues.
4. I practise meditation or relaxation.
5. I withdraw physically from stressful situations when I can.
6. I block out one day or half a day per month in my diary just to spend exactly as I want.
7. I allow myself a good read every day with a novel that takes all my attention.
8. I give myself breaks and treats when I need them.
9. I practise being quiet and avoiding the centre of attention.
10.
11.
Etc.

Score one point for each of 1–9 that you ticked. Score two points for each of 10 onwards.

If you scored more than seven points than you may get stressed up on occasions, but at least you do have some ways of giving yourself a break now and then.

If you scored less than seven points, don't you think you should be doing something about this?

Step 2: Treats

Treats are the rewards and gifts you give yourself. 'I'll just have a little something now' you say, and quite right too. Many busy managers and leaders come to over-rely on particular sources of 'treats' – especially alcoholic drinks after work – and being able to treat yourself properly is about taking care of yourself in all sorts of ways. This includes an ability to reward and pamper yourself at appropriate times – at the end of a hard day, in the middle of a knotty problem, when all seems gloomy and hopeless. Treats are usually little things that give great pleasure – taking a break, a walk in the park, phoning a friend and so on.

The secret of managing stress successfully is by being able to 'pleasure' yourself without guilt in many different ways. Does that sound a bit self-indulgent? Even indecent? Well, that is a problem. The Victorian work ethic encouraged people to split off their enjoyment and pleasures in life and keep them apart from the stern rectitude and selfless duty required at work. Some of us seem to have inherited this guilt about enjoying ourselves at work.

If you want to work hard and continue to enjoy rather than to destroy yourself, you need to take your pleasures seriously: *there is no incompatibility between enjoyment and productivity*!

Write down at least five ways in which you take care of yourself at work and treat yourself well:

1.

2.

3.

4.

5.

Were you able to manage that?

If not, why not? Women managers and leaders may often be juggling work, career development and family commitments and may not have the time or energy to treat themselves. Some men are bad at treating themselves and rely on women to be the 'emotional specialists' – and so on.

What's your pattern?

It might be good fun to do some research among your friends or colleagues. If you can enquire in the right spirit, it may throw up a surprising catch – there are all sorts of possibilities for treating yourself.

Follow-up

The resources for the previous Activity will also be of relevance here, and the next two Activities will also help you with this quest. Take care.

Relaxation

Emotional resilience

When humans first evolved, we were constantly faced with threats in the form of dangerous animals, warring bands and so on. The reaction to these threats was to get rid of them – by fight or flight. To help with these reactions, the human body (like that of animals) prepared itself in various ways. These include an increased rate of breathing, a raised blood pressure, faster heart beat, greater flow of blood to muscles and other physiological responses.

Today's managers and leaders, finding themselves in threatening situations, will also resort to fight and flight and, although these stressful situations are very different from those of our ancestors, the body's response is similar. In these situations we experience marked increases in pulse rate, blood pressure, breathing, etc.

Unfortunately, these body responses, although excellent for dealing with wild beasts, don't help us much in coping with organizational problems. As we usually don't actually fight or run, all the physiological changes are channelled into other effects, causing irritable behaviour and stress. In the longer term, the body's responses to stressful and threatening situations gradually build up, with serious and lasting consequences.

To cope with the physical symptoms, many people in stressful jobs resort to chemical aids such tranquillizers. However, these can hardly be recommended as a long-term solution; what is needed is an internal method of coping with stress reactions. There are many, ancient and modern, approaches to managing your own stress, often associated with specific philosophies or religions, for example, the many forms of yoga and meditation.

The activity here is not associated with any particular belief system, but is a synthesis of the common elements of a number of approaches to relaxation.

More than with most of the activities in this book, you need to repeat this activity over a longish period of time for it to work at its best.

Activity

Step 1

Find a quiet place where you can sit down comfortably in your own space. It is important to be fairly straight and upright. Although some people like to sit cross-legged on the floor, this is not essential and you may be more comfortable in a chair. In this case, sit with both feet on the ground, back straight, head up. Don't be *too* comfortable – don't fall asleep.

Step 2

When you are comfortable, close your eyes and consciously relax all your muscles, starting at the top of your head and moving down through your body to the tips of your toes. Do this gradually, trying to sense each part of the body and muscle groups.

If you have difficulty in doing this, tell yourself that you becoming more and more relaxed, that you are going deeper … and deeper … and deeper. It is often helpful to imagine yourself going down, in a lift, on an escalator; in warm water, to the bottom of the sea.

Step 3

Breathe through your nose, and listen to your own breathing. As you become more relaxed, you will notice your breathing become slower, shallower and more restful. Notice that at the bottom of each breath (i.e. after breathing out) there is a pause before you begin to breathe in again.

Step 4

When you have noticed these pauses, start counting backwards from ten to one. Count thus: breathe out: TEN: breathe in: breathe out: NINE: breathe in: breathe out: EIGHT; etc. Count in this way from ten down to one, then back up from one to ten, down from ten to one, and so on.

Step 5

Stray thoughts may come into your head while you are breathing/counting. Don't worry about this; just let the thought come, don't dwell on it, let it go. Then go back to TEN and start counting again. Don't worry if you never reach ONE, especially in the early days.

Step 6

Continue breathing/counting in this way for 15–20 minutes (although 10 minutes may be easier to start with) at least once a day; twice is better. Keep a watch or clock handy, and check if you wish (otherwise keep your eyes closed). When you finish, remain sitting quietly for a few minutes, then stand up slowly.

Follow-up

This activity is one that should be incorporated into your lifestyle to be of maximum benefit.

You might like to carry the simple technique given in this activity a stage further. There are numerous books, tapes, aromatic oil kits and all sorts of wonderful things that aim to help you to relax. Herbert Benson's *The Relaxation Response* (New York: Avon Books, 2000) was a groundbreaking book and is still deservedly a best seller.

Another favourite, with over one million copies sold, is Lawrence LeShan's *How to Meditate*, again published over 20 years ago but still going strong (London: Little Brown, 1999). More recent, and complemented by two CDs, study cards and a beginner's instruction book, is Joseph Goldstein and Sharon Salzberg's *Insight Meditation Kit: A Step-by-Step Course on How to Meditate* (Louisville, CO: Sounds True Audio, 2002).

Finally, one which caught our eye – *Belly Dancing: For Health and Relaxation* by Tina Hobin and Kristyna K'ashvili (London: Duckworth, 1994) – the very thought of introducing this to clients works wonders.

Fitness

Learning area	Emotional resilience

There is a steadily growing recognition of the essential link between physical fitness, on the one hand, and mental alertness, high morale, motivation and general effectiveness, on the other. To be the manager or leader that you really can be, you need to keep yourself fit.

In this activity, we simply stress the importance of this aspect of self-development, and make some suggestions about the sources of further guidance.

Fashions in fitness come and go, and new books reflect these ideas appear regularly. Find a regime of regular exercise which suits you – your personality, lifestyle, age, present level of fitness and so on – and build it into your work and life. This will not only make you feel physically better, it will have a payoff in all areas of your work – particularly where you are in stressful, demanding situations. Put it this way: can you afford not to be fit?

There are many simple ways to improve your fitness – one US study showed that executives who climbed just 50 steps each day reduced their risk of heart disease by almost half. Giving up using lifts, walking two miles each day, going for a swim twice a week, will all make a difference. Just start doing something.

Follow-up

Many organizations now have keep-fit facilities; most local authorities offer fitness activities; some colleges put on programmes designed specifically for certain age groups or lifestyles and you will find always find plentiful books and workout videos in your local bookshop.

Activity 34, *Be your own personal trainer*, will give you lots more ideas for getting fitter.

Manage Your Feelings

Learning areas	**Emotional resilience:** Social skills: Self-knowledge

Being aware of one's own feelings helps us to become more emotional resilient. Awareness is a first requirement for control, yet bottling up natural feelings – keeping a stiff upper lip – is not always a good thing.

Open expression of feelings can be beneficial to the individual and can lead to more open interpersonal relationships. This must be qualified. If you are just 'dumping' anger or distress on others or if there are strong organizational norms that make such expression taboo, this is unlikely to have good outcomes. We express feelings by what we say, but also significant is the way we say it, and the non-verbals of facial expression, gesture and posture.

This activity will give you practice at becoming aware of, and expressing, your feelings – and also at identifying the feelings as expressed by others. The aim is to have choice in how you handle your feelings. Do you bottle up or freely express? These alternatives may be appropriate to particular situations; but bottle your feelings up, and you'll have to express them somehow, somewhere. It is best by far if you are in charge of this expression.

Activity

Do Steps 1 and 2 with a partner – a colleague spouse or friend, or even a small group of four or five persons.

Step 1

This focuses on the expression of feelings through the *way we speak*, as opposed to *what we say*.

Copy this list of feelings on to small cards or pieces of paper – one feeling per piece.

Excited	Patronizing	Angry
Depressed	Sarcastic	Bored
Happy	Tired	Affectionate
Enthusiastic	Disliking	Frightened
Threatened	Curious	Superior
Preoccupied	Cautious	Interested

Now shuffle the cards and select one at random. Imagine that your partner has just said or done something that evokes the feeling on the card in you. Get into that feeling and then demonstrate it in how you say the following:

'*Well, now, there are lots of implications in this.*'

Your partner now guesses what feeling you are trying to convey. If they get it wrong, try again.

Take it in turns to express and guess feelings. Do this for at least five rounds.

Now discuss this experience. Were some feelings particularly easy or difficult to express? Why do you think this is? How accurate were you and your partner ability in interpreting feelings? What are the implications of your answers?

Step 2

Now try the same activity, this time with the non-verbal expression of feelings, such as by facial expression, gesture, body posture, etc.

Follow the same procedure as for Step 1, except that instead of expressing feelings through the sentence, 'Well, now, there are lots of implications in this', do so in any way you wish but *without words.*

As before, take turns and then discuss.

Step 3

Use Table A31.1 to keep a 'feelings log' from your everyday activities. Examine the feelings you experience from events at work and identify how you *think* you expressed them, then check this out with the other people who were present.

Think of some events – meetings, discussions, episodes – from the last few weeks. Write down your feelings on each particular occasion in Column 1, then think about why you felt that way, and note that briefly in Column 2.

In Column 3, answer yes or no to the question 'Did you express your feelings?' Explain your decision to express your feelings or not in Column 4. Finally, use Column 5 to check out with the other people involved in the situation whether

Table A31.1 The feelings log

1 Your feelings at a particular time	2 What caused these feelings?	3 Did you express your feelings?	4 If not, why not? If so, how did you express them?	5 Check with others. How did they think you were feeling? Why?

they correctly perceived your feelings or not. Ask them what *they* thought you were feeling, and why. Compare this with your own perception of your feelings, and the way in which you did or did not express them.

When you have made a number of entries in the feelings log, look for patterns or repeating themes. Ask yourself these questions:

- Do certain types of events lead to certain feelings?
- What different causes lead to a particular feeling?
- Which feelings do I express, and which do I not?
- Why?
- When do I express feelings? When don't I?
- To whom do I express them? To whom don't I?
- Do people sense some of my feelings, but not others?
- Are some people more accurate in their perception of my feelings than others?

Follow-up

A great deal of attention has been given to the idea of 'emotional intelligence' in recent years and this has emerged as a key area of capability for managers and leaders.

Daniel Goleman has made this his own domain, and his *Emotional Intelligence* (New York: Bantam Books, 2005) is the basic primer. Together with Richard Boyatsis and Anne McKee, Goleman has also produced the more focused *The New Leaders: From the Art of Leadership to the Science of Results* (New York: Little, Brown, 2002).

Gael Lindenfield presents a seven-step 'emotional healing strategy' in *Emotional Confidence: Simple Steps to Manage Your Feelings* (London: Harper Collins/Thorsons, 2000; an audio cassette version is also available). The same author has written a number of related books, including one specifically on *Managing Anger* (London: Harper Collins/Thorsons, 2000) and the more general *Gael Lindenfield's Self-esteem Bible* (London: Element Books/Thorsons, 2004).

Lorraine Bell's *Managing Intense Emotions and Overcoming Self-destructive Habits* (Hove: Brunner-Routledge, 2003) is a self-help manual with a number of 'sessions' for people for whom these present significant challenges. And specifically for men is *Nothing's Wrong: A Man's Guide to Managing His Feelings*, by David Kundtz (York Beach, ME: Conari Press, 2004).

As you might predict, there are also many websites. To test your EIQ (Emotional Intelligence Quotient), try www.myskillsprofile.com, and the Emotional Intelligence Consortium www.eiconsortium.org specializes in information and research related to emotional intelligence in the workplace.

Stability Zones

The limits of emotional resilience are experienced as loss of control or ability to cope. According to Alvin Toffler, we can all cope with huge amounts of change, pressure, complexity and confusion, as long as we have some 'stability zones'. These are oases of stability in our lives that serve as anchors or retreats to allow us to cope with the chaos and instability of other areas.

Stability zones can be **Ideas**, **Places**, **People**, **Things** or **Organizations**. Working out where *your* stability zones are (or could be), and then cultivating them, will develop your emotional resilience and capacity to cope with pressure.

- **Ideas** may be deeply felt religious beliefs, or a strong commitment to a particular philosophy, political ideology, or cause.
- **Places** as stability zones can be large scale (like your country) or small scale (like your street or room). These are your personal spaces where you feel at home, perhaps where you grew up or spent happy times.
- Particular **People** provide a main source of stability for many of us. These are valued and enduring relationships with family members, long-standing friends or trusted colleagues.
- **Things** as stability zones are favourite, familiar and comforting possessions. These can be clothes – that old shirt or pair of shoes – family heirlooms, items from childhood, treasured gifts or mementoes. **Things** can also be houses or books or cars. Lots of things.
- **Organizations** which provide stability include the work organization itself, professional bodies membership institutes, clubs, communities of practice – any form of organizational belonging with which we identify.

Many stability zones overlap categories: home, for example, combines place, people, things and organizations. Given one good stability zone, we can cope with many sources of change and instability.

Activity

Work through the following questions, making notes of your answers.

Step 1: What are YOUR stability zones?

Think through each of the five areas of ideas, places, things, people, and organizations. Note specific anchors where you find stability under:

◼ Ideas?

_____

_____

_____

◼ Places?

_____

_____

_____

◼ People?

_____

_____

_____

◼ Things?

_____

_____

_____

■ Organizations?

_____

_____

_____

Step 2: How stable are your stability zones?

Look through your stability zones from Step 1. Are they sound and secure? Can you count on them staying the same? Will they last?

■ Ideas?

■ Places?

■ People?

■ Things?

■ Organizations?

Step 3: How satisfied are you with your stability zones?

Work through the following and make a few notes:

■ Are the ideas, places, things, people and organizations that you depend on enough for you?

_____

_____

_____

■ Are there any changes you want to make in your stability zones?

_____

_____

_____

■ Do you need to find some new ones?

_____

_____

_____

■ How could you work to develop your ideas, look after your possessions, care better for the people that are important to you?

_____

_____

_____

Follow-up

The idea of personal stability zones for 'coping with tomorrow' is in Alvin Toffler's *Future Shock* (London: Pan, 1973).

Career Anchors by Ed Schein (San Francisco: Jossey-Bass/Pfeiffer, 1993) is helpful for sorting out the important elements and values in your career. Since the book itself was published, a number of complementary works have appeared, including *Career Anchors: Self-assessment* and *Career Anchors: Participant Workbook* (both San Francisco: Jossey-Bass/Pfeiffer, 2006).

Bruce Eimer and Moshe Torem suggest *Ten Simple Solutions for Coping with Uncertainty* (Oakland, CA: New Harbinger Publications, 2005) to 'help readers feel safe and stay calm when life changes or uncertain times make them feel vulnerable or anxieties start to hamper their daily activities'.

On a broader front, Mike Pedler and Tom Boydell's *Managing Yourself* (London: Lemos and Crane, 1999) suggests, via lots of activities and illustrations, that the healthy life is founded on knowing and valuing yourself. In a similar vein is Kees Locher and Jos van der Brug's *Workways: Seven Stars to Steer By* (Stroud: Hawthorne Press, 1997). Angus Jenkinson's *From Stress to Serenity* (Forest Row, Sussex: Sophia Books, 2003) provides a deep and somewhat spiritual approach to handling stress.

The Virtual Revolution

We now live in world dominated by e-mail, websites and personal computers, and apparently more time on the Internet than watching TV. The *virtual revolution* is said to be the most significant since the 18th century industrial revolution in terms of how it affects society, the economy and how our own lives are structured.

We are now in the midst of a revolution which is transforming how we work and live. There are three aspects to the virtualization of business, organization and work:

■ Virtual workplaces – the extent of work now done through e-mail, websites, the Internet and intranets, teleworking, dispersed teams, remote relationships and so on.

■ Virtual organizational dynamics – many organizational processes now work virtually – access to organizational members, information, resources; the monitoring of work relationships and personal performance; the functioning of value chains and networks, procurement and delivery of goods and services, including the management of intellectual and knowledge products, is done through IT-mediated relationships and systems in a virtually transparent world.

■ Virtually located organizations – these are increasingly 'present' in the world through websites, portals, and search engines. Organizations are increasingly electronically connected to suppliers, customers, clients and owners/sponsors.

Those who survive and thrive in this era will be those who understand it best and have the personal strategies to deal with it. Here are some ideas to help you into this position.

Step 1: Reviewing your virtual work style

Leaders and managers have been to some extent 'office workers', but the office is changing dramatically. Here is a progression of 'office types' – how are you situated now?

1. Private or shared office.
2. Open plan – fixed work space in a large room, with or without partitions and bookable private meeting rooms.
3. Hot desking – no fixed personal location, but temporary work spaces at particular locations – often with a personal mobile set of drawers and laptop docking stations.
4. Café society-style workplaces, with an emphasis on informal meeting spaces – perhaps combined with hot desking.
5. Telecottaging – home-based workstation connected to the organizational intranets, etc.
6. Hypermobile workstyle – mobile working from wherever – trains, planes, cars, hotel foyers, other people's offices, cybercafes, etc.

The rationales for different office arrangements are influenced by fashion and status, as well as efficiency. Many senior managers still have more traditional offices (although sometimes combined with other types).

Consider these questions:

1. What has been the history or pattern of office arrangements over your career?

2. What changes would you like to make to your current arrangements?

3. Do you have a working understanding of all the office arrangements listed above? Do you have the appropriate skills to work with all of them?

You need to be versatile in the kinds of arrangements that you are comfortable with, and can work effectively in.

Step 2: Reviewing your virtual work relationships

How adapted are you to the virtual processes and interactions within your organizations, including your relationship to other people and your access to resources?

Here are some questions to help review this:

1. Who and what do you work with in your organizational setting?

2. What is the mix of face-to-face and virtual interaction?

3. What virtual organizational processes are you hooked into? (virtual meetings, overseeing IT-controlled business processes, working on virtual projects, etc.).

4. How are these changing? (what is the trend to increasing virtualization in your organization?).

5. Where does this leave you? (are you being marginalized, or are trends making you more central to key organizational processes?).

6. What organizational knowledge/information resources do you use, maintain, contribute to?

7. What is happening in terms of the virtualization of your organization's location? Is this expanding or obliterating your personal job/work/role?

Organizations are now 'known' in virtual space through websites and other virtual communication processes. Organizational location is increasingly virtualized and some organisations, such as e-retailers, exist almost entirely in virtual space, selling, delivering and being supplied through electronic management.

Step 3: Positioning yourself

To prepare for the virtual world, look at the following 'To Do' list. Tick any items that apply to you:

- Learn more about what's going on in terms of the further virtualization of my work and my organization.
- Acquire new skills including language/terminology, fluency with packages, on-line and web conferences, databases, etc.
- Get access to more resources including kit, maintenance help and backups, advice, education and learning opportunities.
- Get better and more connections to websites, intranets, special resources, etc.
- Up my virtual presence – get better represented on intrancts, websites, etc., so others can find me.
- Make sure that I'm not in danger of being 'disintermediated', i.e. replaced as a go-between by search engines and websites, etc.

If you have ticked one or more items off this list, then print it off and carry it around with you until you have completed these tasks.

Follow-up

Much has been written about virtual teams and organizations over the past few years. Recommended works include *Virtual and Networked Organizations*, by Philippa Collins (Oxford: Capstone/Wiley, 2002); *Virtual Teams: People Working Across Boundaries with Technology*, by Jessica Lipnack and Jeffrey Stamps (New York: Wiley, 2000); and Deborah Duarte and Tennant Snyder's *Mastering Virtual Teams: Strategies, Tools and Techniques that Succeed* (San Francisco: Jossey-Bass, 2001), which also contains a number of practical checklists and a CD-ROM.

Virtual Teams that Work: Creating Conditions for Virtual Team Effectiveness, edited by Cristina Gibson and Susan Cohen (San Francisco: Jossey-Bass, 2003), is broad-ranging with authors from a variety of disciplines including psychology, sociology, engineering, information technology, political science and economics.

Be Your Own Personal Trainer

Learning areas	**Emotional resilience:** Proactivity: Self-knowledge

Are you stressed out, overworked, feeling tired and out of control?

Then you could benefit from personal fitness training. More than two million people in the UK have engaged in some form of fitness training, and a growing number have their own personal fitness trainer. With busy, busy lives, many of us are too stressed, getting too little sleep, eating too much junk food and not doing enough exercise. You've heard it all before.

The good news is that growing numbers of people are deciding to act and do something for themselves. Lifestyle management starts by looking at how you live your life and deciding what you want to change. Making these changes is not easy, but the paybacks are considerable. Learning new habits of managing your personal fitness not only improves your physical appearance and well-being but also gives more energy, mental sharpness and general self-confidence.

Murray's story

With a big family reunion coming up in the summer, Murray wanted to get fitter and lose weight. With a demanding job and a growing family, Murray's life was full and he had no time to exercise. At 48, and not tall, he was 200 lb and he felt terrible. His parents had been overweight and his father had had diabetes. It was time to do something. But what? He had already tried dozens of different diets.

After talking with his GP, Murray contacted a personal fitness trainer and began to learn things about himself that he had not appreciated before. His trainer asked him to record his activities and consumption over seven days.

This made grim reading. Although Murray thought of himself as eating a healthy diet, his trainer pointed out the lack of fruit and vegetables and the quantities of saturated fat and refined sugar. There were other surprises in this initial diagnosis. Murray knew liquids were important of but did not know that tea, coffee and even Coke were diuretics. 'Most of us are dehydrated for a lot of the time', his trainer said, 'you don't drink enough water'.

After various tests and analyses of Murray's current habits, the trainer helped him set some simple goals for the next ten weeks. They agreed on clear targets including a weight loss of 1 lb per week. Murray protested this at first because he wanted to lose more and faster. 'It's a trap to be too ambitious' insisted the trainer, 'be realistic and you will be able to sustain the effort and the improvement'. The trainer gave Murray diet sheets to follow and prescribed five exercise sessions per week of 30 minutes each.

After ten weeks, with twice-weekly sessions with his trainer, Murray had lost 11 lb and inches from his waist. His pulse rate was down, his metabolism was up and he generally felt better. From being only able to run a few steps, he could now run on a treadmill for 15 or even 20 minutes. There was some way to go to meet all his targets – and he had developed some new ones on the way – but he had made a good start.

Activity

This activity will help you diagnose and act on your personal fitness.

Step 1: Observation

Complete a seven-day log to get a picture of your lifestyle. It is important to collect data before deciding what to do. You can look at anything you want but some of the usual categories are suggested in the chart in Fig. A34.1.

Step 2: Analysis

Looking at your seven-day log, what does it tell you about your lifestyle?
Compare it with the following general health advice.

Diet

A woman with a sedentary job needs 1500–2000 calories per day, a man 2000–2500 (although these vary and depend on many factors, such as your metabolic rate).

	Mon	Tues	Wed	Thurs	Fri	Sat	Sun
Calorie intake – Breakfast – Lunch – Evening							
Portions fruit/veg.							
Caffeine intake							
Units of alcohol							
Cigarettes							
Stress level							
Exercise taken							

Figure A34.1   Lifestyle log

- *Breakfast* is the most important meal of the day – it wakes up your metabolism and powers your brain and body.
- *Water* – drink lots of it – 2.5 litres per day at least – we are mainly composed of water and many common ailments stem from dehydration.
- *Fruit and vegetables.* Try to eat at least five and up to ten 3-oz units of fruit and vegetables per day – cooked or raw, with as wide a range of colours as possible.

■ *Saturated fats*. Reduce these cholesterol-raising fats (mainly animal products – meat, cheese, full-fat milk) and increase *polyunsaturated* fats, which can lower blood cholesterol (mainly fruit and vegetables and oily fish – mackerel, salmon, etc.).

■ *Dietary fibre*. Soluble fibre as found in oats, peas, beans, fruit, etc., can also lower cholesterol in addition to scrubbing out your system.

■ *Variety* is an important word in diet – try writing down all the types of food you eat in a week. How many can you list? 10? 20? 30?

Around 30–50 types of food is a good target to give you all the vitamins and minerals you need. If you are below this, think about building in more variety, especially from fruit and vegetables where there is now a huge variety available.

Caffeine

One person who complained of dizziness and other symptoms logged her coffee intake and found it was over 20 cups per day. She worked in an office with a free vending machine. Try to limit your tea and coffee intake to 2–3 cups per day – drink water instead or decaffeinated coffee.

Alcohol

Government guidelines suggest a maximum of 2–3 units per day for women and 3–4 for men. A unit is a half pint of ordinary beer or a small glass of wine or spirits. Try to have at least two alcohol-free days a week.

Cigarettes

You know the advice on this. Retirement annuities are much higher for smokers.

Stress

This is more difficult to diagnose on your own because it has many possible symptoms – raised pulse levels, tiredness, irritability, inability to sleep and so on. If you have noted any signs like these on your chart then you should plan to reduce your stress levels. Common methods for this are exercise, yoga or meditation – but any way that you can relax and slow down – by reading, listening to music or doing the Activities in this book – will help.

Exercise

The recommendation is for 30 minutes of moderate exercise five times per week. Moderate exercise is that which gets you slightly out of breath, slightly sweaty and warm. There are two basic types of exercise – resistance training and cardiovascular work. Resistance training involves building muscular tone, strength and endurance by exercising against some sort of resistance, for example using weights (e.g. hand-held weights, weights machines or your own body weight). Cardiovascular work or aerobic training (improving the efficiency of oxygen intake to your body) involves fast walking, jogging, running, biking or swimming to raise the pulse and get your body working harder than normal.

The best form of exercise is the exercise that you enjoy taking.

NB. If you have known health problems, or are seriously overweight, talk with your GP before undertaking any radical changes of diet or exercise. Radical lifestyle changes are not recommended in any case – slow and easy is the best way – but it might be a good idea to have a check-up anyway. Get clearance and encouragement to go ahead, and then you can go back to your doctor and show them later how well you have done.

Step 3: Setting goals and creating an action plan

Setting goals for health and lifestyle improvement is where personal trainers can be most helpful. The key thing is not to be too ambitious and avoid quick-fix diets and crash programmes of exercise.

To make your plan work, it has to fit with your current lifestyle. If you attend a lot of business dinners, what's your strategy for handling this aspect of your life? If you have small children or work long hours, how will you fit in five 30-minute slots of exercise?

Set some sensible longer term targets and then put some goals for the next week (see Fig. A34.2). Look for positive changes and set simple goals. If you had three glasses of wine last night, then have a night off tonight and buy yourself some delicious sparkling water!

Step 4: Reviewing progress

A weekly planner is good because it gives you a manageable target period for diet and exercise. At the end of each week, note any divergences from that week's plan and, before making your plan for the next week, decide if there are any modifications you need to make in order to hit your targets.

It nearly always helps if you have someone to discuss this with. Perhaps you can recruit your partner or someone at work to join you in this lifestyle management change?

Celebrate success when you hit your targets. Give yourself a treat that does not ruin your plan.

	Mon	Tues	Wed	Thurs	Fri	Sat	Sun
Calorie intake – Breakfast – Lunch – Evening							
Portions fruit/veg.							
Caffeine intake							
Units of alcohol							
Cigarettes							
Stress level							
Exercise taken							

Figure A34.2   Action plan

Follow-up

There are many sources of useful advice and help on personal fitness. Locally, you can talk to your GP – which you should certainly do if you have health problems or are very overweight. Other local professionals who can help include registered personal trainers and the staff at your local gymnasium or sports centre. Here are some other places to start, including a free offer from the British Heart Foundation (BHF).

Books

So You Want to Lose Weight ... for Good is a booklet compiled by experienced nutritionists and is available free from the BHF (address given below). The BHF also publish another free booklet – *Physical Activity for Weight Loss. All Round Fitness,* by Oliver Barteck (London: Konemann, 1999) is an excellent book translated from the original German which features exercises and activities for warming up, strength, mobility and endurance as well as for losing weight. It has lots of pictures and illustrations to show you how to do the exercises and the effects they have.

Other books include Bernis Shrosbree's *Inspired: It's Like Having Your Own Personal Trainer* (Hayden Publishing, 2004); John Shepherd's *Ultrafit: Your Personal Trainer* (A & C Black, 2004); and the all-encompassing *The Real Woman's Personal Trainer: A Goal-by-Goal Programme to Lose Fat, Tone Muscle, Perfect Posture and Boost Energy for Life,* by Sam Murphy (London: Kyle Kathie, 2005).

If you prefer a DVD then there is *Joanna Hall's 28 Day Total Body Plan* (2004).

Useful addresses

1. The British Heart Foundation
   14 Fitzhardinge Street, London W1H 4DH, tel. 020 7935 0185; www.bhf.org.uk/.
2. Association of Personal Trainers
   Suite 2, 8 Bedford Court, London WC2E 9LE, tel. 020 7836 1102.
3. National Register of Premier Trainers and Therapists
   Parade House, 70 Fore Street, Trowbridge, Wiltshire BA14 8HQ, tel. 01225 253555.

Acknowledgement

This Activity was created with the help of Sophie Barraclough, a Personal Fitness Trainer, working from Huddersfield.

Who's the Boss?

In complex, interdependent social systems, decisions are very rarely ours to take alone. Decisions about changes, decisions on problems, decisions about where to go and what to do are all made and often negotiated with those who are most concerned.

But who is really the 'boss' on the important decisions that affect your life? It should be you; and you should be able to choose the team to help you make good decisions and not hold you back. Some people will both give to and take from you; others will only take; their impact is largely destructive. The former cause you to grow and strengthen from your interaction with them; the latter weaken you.

This activity offers you an opportunity to select the team, and to be the boss, and even to remove those people whose influence is not helpful.

Activity

Step 1: The decision

Choose a decision you have to make in the near future. Don't choose a decision you have already made because the issue needs to be 'live'. The decision chosen should not be a simple choice between clear alternatives (e.g. choosing a new car), but a complex matter involving others and their feelings and relationships, and affecting a number of areas of your life (e.g. making a decision affecting your children, changing your job or some other aspect of your life).

Step 2: The board

Use the 'boardroom' diagram in Fig. A35.1 to think about this decision. Write in the name of the 'directors' who have a say in the making of this decision. Choose the people in your life who you trust or value to be your directors. Six to twelve is a good number. Put their initials on the chairs round the table.

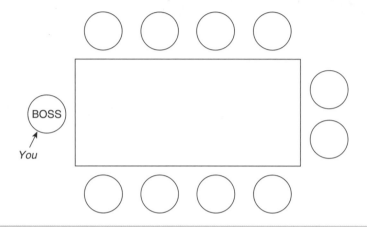

Figure A35.1   The boardroom

Step 3: The advice

Next to each of the 'directors' jot down notes on the advice that you think he or she would give on this decision.

Step 4: Weighing the advice

Take a good look at this advice. Of each director in turn, ask yourself:

■ Whose interest do they have at heart in making points, theirs or mine?

■ Is she or he interested in getting a good decision or not?

Step 5: Confirming the team

As the boss, you take the decisions. You can also revise the management team, although you can't remove people just because you don't like them. You need to distinguish between liking a person and concern for a good decision. They have a right to be there even if you don't like their advice.

Take a look at your management team:

(a) Are you really the boss?

(b) Are there any directors who shouldn't be there?

(c) Have you got enough advice of the right kind? Could you use a new director? Perhaps to replace one of your less useful ones?

Follow-up

This activity is putting you in charge of the important decisions in your life. If you and your boss sometimes seem to have difficulty in appreciating each other, try Activity 39, *Managing upwards*, which makes a good follow-up.

The Managing Upwards Pocketbook, by Patrick Forsyth (Alresford: Management Pocketbooks, 2002) and Patti Hathaway and Susan Schubert's *Managing Your Boss* (London: Kogan Page, 1993) offer strategies and techniques for improving things. *Managing Your Boss*, by Christie Kennard (Aldershot: Gower, 1996) is an alternative, and if you are in a hurry you could turn to Sandi Mann's *Managing Your Boss in a Week* (London: Hodder Arnold, 2002).

If you are interested in literally being your own boss, *Be Your Own Boss*, by John Whiteley (London: How To Books, 2000) may help. For other aspects of running your own business, try *The 'Which' Guide to Starting Your Own Business: How to Make a Success of Going it Alone* (London: Which? Books, 2003) and Michael Becket's *The 'Daily Telegraph' Small Business Guide to Starting Your Own Business* (London: Pan, 2003).

The last word – or picture – on bosses is provided by Dilbert in Scott Adams' *The Boss: Nameless, Blameless and Shameless* (Boxtree, 1998). This appears to be out of print – but the very title of the same author's *Dilbert and the Way of the Weasel: A Guide to Outwitting Your Boss, Your Coworkers, and the Other Pants-Wearing Ferrets in Your Life* (New York: Harper Collins, 2003; an audiobook version is also available) perhaps speaks for itself!

Practising Change

Proactivity: Sensitivity to events: Emotional resilience

There is a lot of blather talked about change. On the one hand, in some organizations change has become an unquestioned necessity, an argument to influence people, even a fetish. It has become a treadmill which leads to the demand for yet more of it. And there are many questions about change: does it always lead to better products or services? Are the changes made around here for the benefit of customers and users? Have previous changes been successful?

On the other hand, the complexities of life put a premium on personal and organizational flexibility. To get the best out of people, jobs, teams and organizations, we all need to become familiar with change processes and their effects. Leaders and managers do not just 'implement' changes (whatever their bosses may like to think); on many occasions they actively resist changes or seek to minimize their effects. To implement or resist, we need first to understand.

This activity offers some experiments for learning about change and its effects. The aim is to practise change on yourself. What you learn as a result of the risks you take and the changes you experience will prepare you for changes imposed on you and over which you have no control. It will also prepare you for planning change with other people – how it feels, what reactions to expect and how to cope with them.

Activities

Experiment 1: Eating a new food

The next time you go to a restaurant, or even the staff restaurant if the menu is varied enough, eat a new dish which you haven't tried before.

Before eating – note down

■ What are your expectations about the experience you are about to have?

_____

_____

_____

■ It is going to be pleasant or unpleasant, exciting or stressful?

_____

_____

_____

■ What are your feelings as you approach the food?

_____

_____

_____

While eating

■ Concentrate solely on eating, especially the first mouthful. Chew slowly, don't talk, and don't be distracted from the food.

After eating – note down

■ How does this compare with your normal approach to food?

_____

_____

_____

■ How much of a risk did you take?

_____

_____

_____

■ What did you gain as a result of your investment?

_____

_____

_____

■ What did you learn about changing to the unfamiliar?

_____

_____

_____

Experiment 2: Changing your surroundings

Choose a room where you spend considerable time. If you have an office then this might be best, but any familiar room will do. This experiment involves rearranging the furniture, including taking down pictures, removing decorations or putting some new ones up.

Before rearranging – note down

■ Where else could the major pieces of furniture go?

■ What other layout is possible?

■ What alterations could be made to the decorations?

Rearranging

■ Note carefully where you are putting things in your new arrangement.

After rearranging – note down

■ How comfortable do you feel now? (Allow at least a few hours before changing again.)

■ What effect does the new layout have on you and your actions? What are you doing differently?

■ How do other people react to your new layout? (Try and arrange for as many as possible to view and comment on the change.)

■ What have you learned about the effects of physical surroundings?

■ What have you learned about change and its effects on behaviour?

If you learned something useful from this experiment, why not try another variation? How long is it since you looked at the fixtures and fittings of your managerial or leadership practice and considered a spring-clean or rearrangement?

Experiment 3: Changing your image

'Image management' is personal public relations. Try a few changes of image and watch for the results. For this experiment, take three aspects of yourself that have an obvious impact on the outside world, namely your styles of:

■ dress
■ writing
■ greeting.

Dress

Choose a simple change of dress. Leave your tie off or wear a hat. Put on a formal suit if you don't usually wear one; or try casual dress if you usually wear a suit. Embellish your appearance with accessories such as scarves, handkerchiefs, brooches.

As with all these experiments take careful notes – before, during and after – of:

- how you feel beforehand
- how you feel during the introduction and implementation of the change
- how other people react to you
- what you learn about yourself and the effects of change.

Writing

Change your writing style – somehow. Are you a brief or lengthy writer? Are you conciliatory or aggressive in style? Serious or jokey?

Whatever you are or whatever your usual practice, try a change, e.g. write some humour into committee minutes.

Ask yourself the same questions as for 'Dress'.

Greeting

This is a surprisingly powerful communicator. First, you must recognize your usual routine. Do you greet everyone from cleaner to CEO with the same effusiveness or brevity? Do you sneak into work avoiding everyone's eyes?

Select a new approach and try it out. Give your friends a brief and businesslike greeting and chat at length with the cleaners. Buttonhole the CEO in the lift and pass the time of day.

Ask yourself the same before, during and after questions.

For all these experiments, give yourself a few minutes of peace and reflection to extract the most from the experience.

Experiment 4: An unpleasant situation

This is the most difficult of the experiments and it is therefore recommended to graduates of the earlier ones.

Choose a situation that you know from experience you will probably not enjoy and would normally avoid.

This might be as simple as digging the garden or cleaning the lounge, or it might be more complex, like spending the whole evening on your own in a bar, or deliberately spending some time with a colleague whom you dislike.

Work through the following steps:

1. List some situations that you find unpleasant and try to avoid.

    _____

    _____

    _____

2. Pick one and deliberately put yourself into it.

    _____

    _____

    _____

3. Record your feelings on paper:

    ■ Before:

    _____

    _____

    _____

    ■ During:

    _____

    _____

    _____

    ■ Afterwards:

    _____

    _____

    _____

4. Write a short story changing the outcome of the experience.

    _____

    _____

    _____

5. Identify how much personal responsibility you feel for what happened or did not happen?

_____

_____

_____

Follow-up

If you enjoyed these experiments and learned something about risk taking and the effects of change, generate some ideas for yourself about things you'd like to change – about yourself, about other people.

An early writer on such change was Albert Ellis, who said that there are four ways of handling an intolerable situation, namely change the situation, change your response to it, change yourself or leave the situation (see Activity 26, *Difficult situations*). His *A Guide to Rational Living* (Wilshire Publications, 1975) is still going strong after 25 years, or you might prefer a more recent title such as *Rational Emotive Therapy: It Works for Me – It Can work for You* (Amherst: Prometheus Books, 2004).

Different approaches can be found in Cynthia Scott and Denis Jaffe's *Managing Personal Change* (Crisp Publications, 1989) and David Noer's *Breaking Free: A Prescription for Personal and Organizational Change* (San Francisco: Jossey-Bass, 1996).

Action Planning

Proactivity: Analytical skills

Action planning is a key part of doing and learning. With small tasks it is semi-automatic – 'next time this happens, I'll do it this' – often without verbalizing or making it conscious. With bigger problems, automatic systems are rarely adequate. Sometimes, we jump into action before we have done sufficient thinking, and miss something important (although, as Activity 14, Decision making, points out, sometimes action comes *before* planning).

An action plan involves setting targets for accomplishing an action. Part of this is establishing quality standards and also time deadlines. Once agreed or written down, your action plan becomes a commitment. Your action plan commits you to a course of action which you will achieve to a certain standard or by a certain date. It is this *commitment* that is one of the most important aspects of an action plan. Planning without commitment is waste.

Activity

This activity follows an action planning sequence with a worked example. Choose your own issue to plan for and work it through in parallel. There are five stages:

1. setting goals
2. establishing sub-goals
3. target dates
4. resources/methods
5. standards.

Or, if you prefer, you can use a short version, stages 1–3.

Step 1

Draw up a chart upon which to detail your action plan. It should have five vertical columns (three if you are using the short method) and look something like Table A37.1.

Table A37.1 Action Plan Chart

Goals	Sub-goals	Target dates	Resources/ methods	Standards

Step 2

Choose a task or an issue that you want to act on or change. It does not have to be a big one. Choose something you are working on now or, perhaps, are about to start on.

If you are the sort of person who makes lists, you should have little difficulty in choosing a task – you will have a mental task list already. If you don't usually make lists, try doing one now.

For example, suppose you are asked to clear your desk in preparation for a top priority job coming in a month's time:

1.   List all the things you would have to do in order to get your desk clear by then.

_____

_____

_____

_____

_____

2. Now choose the *most difficult* task on that list.

Write your task in the left-hand column of the Action Plan Chart.

Step 3

Large tasks tend to look impossible; which gives us every opportunity to avoid them. Setting sub-goals breaks up the main task into manageable proportions. Questions that might throw up sub-goals are:

■ What are the ways in which I could attain my goal?
■ What is involved in this task?

The example worked through here is *Appraising the Work Team*:

■ *Major goal*: Annual appraisals of the work team members
■ *Sub-goals*:
   (a) Memo reminding all concerned of annual appraisal.
   (b) Interviews with: Rose Smith; Maria Correlli; George Evans; Helga Martin; David Salmon.
   (c) Complete paperwork and circulate for agreement.
   (d) Make returns to human resources.
   (e) Make individual action plans for any development needs arising.

Work your chosen goal into sub-goals and put them in the second column of the Action Plan Chart.

Step 4

Setting target dates for your sub-goals first and then estimate the likely date for your overall goal. You may have a final deadline already, in which case you will have to work backwards to plan your sub-goal deadlines.

Fill in target completion dates on your Action Plan Chart. Remember these are your deadlines – failure to achieve them requires explanation – to yourself or to others.

If you're using the short Action Plan, you are now complete. Read the next two steps to see what isn't in your plan.

Step 5

The resources and methods column contains the answers the questions:

■ How am I going to tackle this problem?
■ What alternative courses of action are open to me?
■ What assistance do I need and what can I get?

In our example, resources include:

(a) Appropriate documentation from HR.
(b) HR notes on appraisal interviewing.
(c) Any other useful resources, e.g. training films, checklists, tips, etc.?
(d) Heather (source of advice)

Methods include:

(a) Circulating via intranet where appropriate and possible.
(b) Personal interviews.

In completing the resources and methods column, you may discover that you need to acquire more help before proceeding. If so, this becomes a sub-goal preceding the others.

Step 6

Now add some standards in the last column. These can be quantitative – clear measures that will demonstrate achievement of the goal or sub-goal; often they are qualitative measures which give you an idea or picture of when a task is completed satisfactorily.
    By now you should have an Action Plan Chart, as in Table A37.2.

Step 7

Subject your Action Plan Chart to a critical appraisal. Perhaps you can ask someone who knows about you and the task to help. Examples of searching questions are:

■ Is this goal really important for your department?
■ Will these sub-goals lead to achievement of the main goal?
■ Can that time target be shortened?
■ Will those performance standards tell you how well you're doing?

Table A37.2 Completed action plan chart

1. Goals	2. Sub-goals	3. Target completion dates	4. Resources/ methods	5. Standards
1. Appraising the work section		31 January		Sub-goal 2:
				1. Develop personal, private and confidential climate
			Resources:	
	1. Memo to all concerned	4 January	1. Documentation (personnel)	2. End each interview only after:
	2. Interviews:		2. Appraisal notes (last course)	(a) got all information
	Rose Smith	18 January	3. Anything else in personnel, films, etc.	(b) I feel I've improved relationship
	Maria Correlli	19 January		
	George Evans	20 January		(c) each interviewce has said all; been satisfied or agreed a course of action
	Helga Martin	21 January		
	David Salmon	22 January	4. Jack Williamson	
	3. Complete documentation and circulate	22 January		
			Methods:	
	4. Make returns to personnel	29 January	Internal post	Sub-goal 3:
			Personal interviews (1½hrs each)	Seek *commitment* rather than mere compliance
	5. Make individual action plans on any identified training needs	Say, by 1 March		
				Sub-goal 4: Ensure correctness to avoid return of documents
				Sub-goal 5: Action plans to conform to specification

Follow-up

An Action Plan Chart can give you a clear picture of what is involved in the completion of any complex task and help with the discipline and commitment necessary for its completion.

For interesting views on the limits of rationality, you could browse through Gareth Morgan's *Images of Organisations* (3rd edition, London: Sage, 2006), which shows that linear thinking belongs in the 'organizations as machines' view of the world and that there are many other ways of understanding how things happen.

However, for those of you who never want to see an Action Plan ever again, you might like to try Action Learning – Reg Revans' proposal for helping people work with difficult issues in the company of like-minded colleagues (*ABC of Action Learning*, London: Lemos and Crane, 1999). In action learning you don't just plan, you *do*; and then reflect on what you've done in order to learn.

Imaging

When we 'image' something we intend it to happen; that is the difference between *imaging* and *imagining*. A colleague used to 'think up a parking space' whenever he travelled to the head office building in town. On a particular day that I travelled with him, sure enough there was a vacant space when we got to the appointed spot. Coincidence? "It's never failed yet", he said, matter of factly.

The idea of bringing about reality through thought has been around a long time. Prayer is perhaps the commonest form of this. The power of positive thinking is used by high-performing people in many fields of endeavour to visualize the results they want. In work organizations it is normal to talk about leaders or managers with (or without) *vision*. This is a recognition that for things happen we must first create a picture of what we want to happen. 'What will it look like?' comes even before 'What's in it for me'.

Imaging is the everyday activity of creating a vivid picture of what we want to bring about – at work, in relationships and in ourselves.

Activity

Step 1

Choose a situation, a relationship or an aspect of yourself that you would like to change or influence. You could choose something which came up in the career planning activity (Chapter 3).

Step 2

Think about this aspect of work, relationship or yourself. Try to build up a picture of how you would like it to look:

■ What would be the best picture you could imagine?

_____

_____

_____

_____

_____

■ Now what do you want it to look like?

_____

_____

_____

_____

_____

Visualize the results you want in this situation.

You might find this difficult to visualize. Some people can picture things easily, but others don't. If you are having difficulty, try writing or drawing to help with you imaging:

1. Write down a list of what you'd like to see in that situation, e.g.
   ■ 'I want my relationship with Alice to be more friendly; less "careful"'.
   ■ 'I want to see us finish the Anshan project on time. I see the team celebrating our success in the Victoria'.
   ■ 'I see myself volunteering to lead the same team a new project'.
   ■ Etc.
   Re-visit this list at least once a day for a week – adding to it and embellishing it.
2. Draw a picture (or, for non-drawers, make a collage from by cutting and pasting pictures and images from magazines) of the image of what you want. When you have a picture, re-visit it at least once a day for a week – adding to it and embellishing it.

For example, if I want to change my room, I can cut out from this magazine just the sort of desk I want; I can photograph or draw what I want to keep from my existing things. I can try out all sorts of decors, furniture, plants, equipment, on paper. I can experiment with layout and even ask other people what they think before taking the plunge.

Step 3

When you have a good picture of what you want to bring about, keep thinking about this, bringing it back to mind or taking it out to focus on it from time to time.

Over time, and without planning in detail, your image of what you want will begin to appear through the working of your intuition in the multitude of everyday decisions.

Step 4

For those who lack confidence or who perhaps are put off by the idea of 'tempting fate', it is really just a creative alternative to the managerial stock in trade of planning, i.e. attempting to influence future events. 'Imaging' is perhaps a necessary precursor to planning; it can add some magic to the managerial culture, with all its graphs, printouts and flow charts.

Maintaining an image requires strength and stamina. All too often the vision fades and the magic is lost. One way to sustain yourself is by daily *affirmation*. This is simply saying (or writing down) to yourself a positive statement about yourself and your image. For example, if I were determined to become less irritable and I had an image of myself as smiling and relaxed, I might say, "I, Mike, am becoming more relaxed and smiling every day". If you were imaging a more creative, productive team, you could say, "Every day, in every way, this team is getting more creative and more productive".

Try a suitable positive affirmation, naming yourself or the people or the situation and say it to yourself every day, perhaps out loud, preferably several times, say six. Alternatively, or additionally, you can write down your affirmation. Do this 20 times each day.

If you feel a bit silly 'affirming yourself', think about this: perhaps being able to be silly at times is an important aspect of creativity and of having fun: "I didn't get where I am today without … !".

Follow-up

Having fun is one aspect of 'imaging', but the power in this is not to be taken lightly. Use 'imaging' for good ends, not to denigrate people – and constantly question your definition of 'good' in this situation. If you want more information on this idea, Vaune Ainsworth-Land's 'Imaging and creativity; an integrative perspective' in *Creative Management* (London: Sage, 2001), edited by Jane Henry, gives an introduction. Gareth Morgan's view that we 'co-produce' our worlds in a partnership of our own inner ideas and more outer realities is given full rein in *Imaginisation* (Thousand Oaks, CA: Sage and San Francisco: Berret-Koehler, 1993).

Peter Senge *et al.*'s *The Fifth Discipline Fieldbook: Strategies and Tools for Building a Learning Organisation* (London: Nicholas Brealey, 1994) has a section on collective visualization. Finally, the bookshop self-development shelves are worth a look for texts on different approaches to visualization and achieving the things you want – try, for example, Shakti Gawain's *Creative Visualization* (Novato, CA: New World Library, 2002).

Managing Upwards

Is your working life being ruined by your relationship with your boss?

One of the most persistent complaints of young managers in organizations is about the quality of their bosses. A recent group of senior professionals in a large utility came up with the following grumbles: "My boss …

- is always too busy
- thinks that things manage themselves
- doesn't listen to me
- never gives me feedback
- only criticizes, never praises
- gives me ridiculous deadlines
- has very obvious favourites
- picks on me and finds fault with my work
- is anxious for me not 'to rock the boat'
- wants to pass off any good ideas as their own
- spends most of their time looking upwards and trying to please their boss
- fails to get a fair share of resources for our department

and most of all …

- is not interested in my learning and development."

For professionals and 'knowledge workers', the preferred boss is a senior colleague rather than a supervisor, a mentor rather than an overseer, more of an adviser and consultant than a work allocator and quality controller.

If your boss hasn't got these messages yet – how can you help him or her to work more in this way? And help yourself in the process?

Rosie's tale (Part 1)

Rosie was a graduate engineer just two years out of university and working on what should have been an exciting marine propulsion technology project. But her boss cast a cloud over her working life, and indeed her life in general.

"Even now, three years on, it makes my blood run cold to think about him", she says, "work could have been so different, if he had been a better manager." Tony (her current boss) is such a contrast – he sees his job as enabling his staff to get on with their work and helping them sort out the tasks. He handles all the politics for the department and generally tries to make life easier for staff. "It was unfortunate for me that Derrick was my first experience of having a manager – if it happened to me now I would know what to do – but then I just put up with it."

Derrick did not see himself as a manager at all, he saw himself as a technical specialist. He would say things like, "I'm very lucky because you all get on with what you have to do and I don't have to manage you", but at the same time he would say, "I can't understand why all my staff leave so quickly." The answer to that was because his staff got so fed up with his complete inability to plan or prioritize work, or to give notice of critical jobs. "He would suddenly drop jobs on you that had been on his desk for days and tell you that it was needed tomorrow. Then he wouldn't give you any feedback and you would never really know whether the customer – usually another department – was pleased with the work or not. Naturally people used to leave as soon as they had the opportunity. Tony's staff leave too but that is because he encourages to move on to bigger things and really makes sure that we get developed whilst we're here – it's just totally different."

"Another thing about Derrick was that he was really naive about politics. He was intransigent and would refuse to compromise. It got us – the department – a bad name in the company. The rest of the organization tends to write you off if you don't deliver, and this is disastrous for our careers as well as for the department."

Rosie was infuriated, but she also felt sorry for Derrick; as a manager, he was a duck out of water and his home life didn't sound too good either. Something had to be done.

Activity

If you spend time grumbling about your boss, or you feel that their actions are affecting your effectiveness, perhaps it is time for you to do something about it? This activity will help you to come up with some ideas for action to manage your boss better. You can then go on to read Part 2 of Rosie's Tale to see what she did next.

Step 1: Analysis

Take a close look at your relationship with your boss.

1. First, make a list of all those things that you consider to be good about it, and those that are bad. Consider such things as:

   ■ work allocation
   ■ time for consultations and discussions
   ■ listening
   ■ willingness to share knowledge
   ■ feedback on work done
   ■ information about the organization
   ■ help with tasks
   ■ access to knowledge
   ■ variety of work and access to special projects
   ■ attention paid to personal development and learning
   ■ career development.

Are there any other important aspects to your relationship that you can think of?

2. Second, make a list of those things which you would like your boss to ...

   ■ Stop doing

   _____

   _____

   _____

   _____

   _____

   ■ Start doing

   _____

   _____

   _____

   _____

   _____

■ Continue to do

_____

_____

_____

_____

_____

These three lists are critical and should give you the basis for a conversation with your boss. However, until now this exercise has been risk-free; Step 2 is more testing.

Step 2: Make an appointment

Ask your boss for a private one-hour meeting to discuss your work. It will be helpful to let them have some idea of what you have in mind.

If you have a good relationship with your boss, you could just suggest that they also prepare for the meeting by competing the three lists above about you. You can then work from the lists at the meeting.

If your relationship is less secure, you could say something like:

"I have been thinking about my job performance and have come up with some ideas to improve my effectiveness. As you could help me with some of these things, I'd like the opportunity of talking with you at some length about these."

Step 3 : Negotiation meeting

Whichever way you do it, this is essentially a negotiation. So you should prepare for the meeting as you would for any negotiation:

1. What are your key goals? What do you want to achieve?

_____

_____

_____

_____

_____

2. What do you have to offer the other person? What's in it for them?

_____

_____

_____

_____

_____

3. What is your bottom line for an agreement? What is your 'fall back' – the least you will settle for?

_____

_____

_____

_____

_____

Always have a fall-back goal in mind in case the meeting does not go as planned. This might even be just to get agreement to a further meeting after you have both had chance to reflect.

Step 4: Agreement and review

All good negotiations end with an agreement – and it is usually worth putting it in writing. Tell your boss you will write up the agreed points and send them a copy.

Also, agree a review date to discuss progress after a month or two and put this in your diaries.

If you can manage this, you will become more confident in dealings with your boss. Confidence begets confidence and Step 2, fixing that appointment, may be the critical point in a journey to a better working life for both of you.

So, what did Rosie do next?

Rosie's tale (Part 2)

Rosie got a clue to the way forward one day when she lost her temper. She was handling some requests on expenditure targets but when she took them in to

Derrick, he was busy and said, "Stuff them, I'm not doing that." Rosie knew that Finance's cooperation was essential to the progress of several of their key projects, and she got mad and put her foot down, insisting that they put the figures in. She did most of the work and made sure they were sent them off. Rosie told this story to her four immediate professional colleagues and they decided to act together improve the things they were grumbling about.

The first thing was the team meetings. They weren't proper meetings, but rambling sessions with Derrick from time to time. The team called the next meeting and set an agenda of critical items demanding action which they divided up and prepared in advance. It was immediately obvious that by talking tasks through, people began to understand what each of them was doing and working on. Derrick didn't seem to mind at all – he hated meetings anyway – "You've said more useful things at this meeting than I've heard in the last year" he said.

As the meetings continued with team members taking the chair in turn, the benefits of understanding the whole work of the department began to pay off with a much better sense of joint priorities and targets. Derrick's job was to present each meeting with any new tasks well in advance of their deadlines. After six months of this collective effort, the external perceptions of the department also improved greatly. It was suddenly obvious how much was getting done – and how limited the departmental influence had been before. Derrick was no different but at least one thing in his life had improved.

Follow-up

There is a rich vein of books on this theme, many of which take the view that your boss is basically the problem. The classic *Managing Your Boss* (*Harvard Business Review*, January/February 1980, pp. 92–100), by John Gabarro and John Kotter, is still worth a visit.

Robert Bramsom's *Coping with Difficult Bosses* (London: Nicholas Brealey, 1994) is another example or, if you want to broaden your target, try the more recent *Coping with Toxic Managers … Subordinates, and Other Difficult People*, by Roy Lubit (Upper Saddle River, NJ: Pearson Education, 2004). If you really feel you are suffering, then *I Hate my Boss!: How to Survive and Get Ahead When Your Boss is a Tyrant, Control Freak or Just Plain Nuts*, by Bob Weinstein (New York: McGraw-Hill, 1998) might appeal.

However, this one-sided approach to the problem can be misleading and veer towards the manipulative in terms of the various strategies suggested for dealing with people. A more empathic approach is found in Mike Leibling's *How People Tick: A Guide to Difficult People and How to Handle Them* (London: Kogan Page,

2005). If you feel up to try taking a collaborative approach to the *relationship* between you and your manager. In this context, Mike Pedler and Tom Boydell's *Managing Yourself* (London: Lemos and Crane, 1999) will help, but a more specific text is Jerry Wisinski's *Building a Partnership with Your Boss* (New York: AMACOM, 1999).

Finally, more information about how to do Role Negotiation and why it can be so helpful can be found as Chapter 4 of *The Collected Papers of Roger Harrison* (Maidenhead: McGraw-Hill, 1994, pp. 42–54).

Beyond 'Yes ... But ...'

Learning areas	**Creativity:** Analytical skills: Self-knowledge

Are you familiar with that bad feeling of putting forward a new idea – to the boss or to other authorities – only to find them blocked or rejected without a fair hearing?

How often is the boot on the other foot? How often do you say, "Yes ... but ..." and reject ideas without a fair hearing? It probably happens more than you think, because accepting other people's ideas is difficult.

Activity

Look out for occasions on which you may reject other people's ideas: at meetings, in projects, as part of your day-to-day work with others, ...

Step 1

When you recognize such an occasion, get a pad and pen and write down as many possible reasons as you can think of as to why you reject an idea.

Write them down without qualification, evaluation or discussion. *Be open and honest.* Such a list could include:

- The idea is impractical.
- It's too expensive.
- It's administratively inconvenient.

- It challenges my basic beliefs.
- It will cause a lot of political headaches.
- It involves risks that I am not prepared to take.
- It makes me feel unnecessary, redundant.
- It devalues my ideas or role.
- I just don't like/respect the person putting forward the idea.
- I find it hard to accept that other people in general, or this person in particular, can have better ideas than you.
- It will cause me to lose face, to backtrack on previously stated ideas or beliefs.
- I don't want this other person to take the credit.

Step 2

Look over the reasons you have given. Challenge them. Cross-examine yourself. Imagine you are a barrister challenging a witness (yourself). For example:

- How do you know it's impracticable? Have you tried it? What happened? Why? Why not?
- What do you mean, too expensive? What are the detailed costs and benefits? How could it be done cheaper? It's your job to be able to do this, isn't it?
- Are you sure you are not rejecting this idea because of the person who made it? What would you say if I pointed out that you nearly always reject ideas put forward by this person? Why is this?

And so on.

This technique of self cross-examination is very powerful (it is a particular version of Activity 52, *Conversations with yourself*).

Step 3

What you do next depends on your 'verdict' following self-examination.

Having identified some of the *real* reasons why you are blocking/rejecting an idea, you will need to explore these further – with yourself and with the other people concerned.

Draw up a list of changes that you will make in response to an idea ('I will try, with the others concerned, to *make* the thing practicable, to *cut* its costs, to *overcome* administrative/political difficulties').

Step 4: Active listening

Whatever else you do from now on, practise *active listening* whenever someone is presenting an idea.

Passive listening is paying just enough attention to note matters of interest; *active listening* is making a conscious attempt to work out what the other person is trying to say, expressing your attention and interest, verbally and non-verbally, and generally encouraging the other in getting their ideas across.

Follow-up

A good coverage of active listening can be found in Michael Reddy's *The Manager's Guide to Counselling at Work* (Leicester: British Psychological Society with London: Methuen, 1987; new imprint, Oxford: Blackwell, 2002).

Generating New Ideas

Learning areas	**Creativity:** Analytical skills

Nothing blocks creative problem solving like premature judgements. New solutions and ideas are by definition unusual, so we reject them as nonsensical, impracticable, expensive, unrealistic – the 'Yes … But …' syndrome.

Stereotyping or narrow vision is another common blocker. Used to doing things in certain ways, we close our minds to alternatives, so that after a time they just never occur to us.

Here is a technique designed to generate new ideas and to overcome the blocks to creative thinking. It can be done individually or in a group.

Activity

To get a sense of the idea generating process, here is a simple example.

Step 1

Write down the answer to the following question:

'What are paper clips used for?'

_____

_____

_____

_____

_____

Step 2

Unless you are a relatively fluent and innovative thinker, you may only have generated one or two uses for paper clips. For example, you may have said something about 'holding two or more pieces of paper together'.

Step 3

Now write down, in five minutes, as many *other possible* uses of paper clips as you can think of.

Don't worry how unusual, peculiar, or odd some of these might be. Write them down and keep thinking of more until the five minutes is up.

_____

_____

_____

_____

_____

Step 4

Individual lists will be very different. Groups can usually generate far more ideas per five minutes. You may have come up with between 10 and 30 possible uses;. here is a partial list made grouped by some of the attributes of paper clips – you will be able to add to this:

- hooks: paperhooks; use for unlocking doors
- links: chains
- pins: cocktail sticks, notice pins
- connectors: fuse, contact maker
- bindings: wire, staple
- centres: axles, spindles, spigots
- magnets: picking up light ferrous objects from narrow or bent holes
- piercing tool: punching small holes, stitches, belt holes
- weapon: use as defensively to stab.

The more attributes you see and make use of, the more you overcome the stereotyping problem.

Making the list quickly and forcing the pace helps to overcome the premature evaluation blockage. There just isn't the time for the 'Yes … Buts …'.

Step 5

Now think of a real problem facing you.

Again, without pausing for evaluation, force yourself to list as many possible solutions as you can.

Don't at this stage allow yourself to consider all the implications, pros and cons of each solution. Just get a good list – the longer the better.

_____

_____

_____

_____

_____

Groups are often very effective in generating new ideas. State the problem and have members compete in shouting out possible solutions, which are written up on a flip chart. During this process, it is vital that no evaluation takes place. It is only when ideas are exhausted, and a very full list has been prepared, that careful, considered evaluation should be attempted.

Step 6

Now is the time to evaluate these possible solutions.

Take each in turn, try to remain open-minded about them, consider all the strengths, weaknesses, consequences, requirements and implications.

Follow-up

You will find Activities 16, *Planning change,* and 37, *Action planning,* useful in generating good new ideas. Or you could start with John Townsend's *The Creative Manager's Pocketbook* (Alresford: Management Pocketbooks, 1999).

Brian Clegg and Paul Birch's *Instant Creativity* (London: Kogan Page, 1999) is a good source of many creativity techniques and Tudor Rickards' *Creativity and Problem-solving at Work* (Gower, 1997) is another useful book full of ideas.

Eric Maisel's *Creativity Book* (New York: Jeremy Tarcher/Putnam, 2000) makes a link between creativity as an artist and as an executive. In a similar vein, if you believe that management and leadership really are artistic endeavours then you might enjoy Twyla Tharp's *The Creative Habit: Learn It and Use It for Life* (New York: Simon and Schuster, 2006).

Approaches to Creativity

Learning area	**Creativity**

There are many techniques and approaches to creative problem solving. Here are a few of them:

- *Draw the problem*:
  Whether or not it is a visual or spatial problem, represent it somehow as a picture or cartoon. Be as uninhibited as you can.
  Now, consider possible solutions to the problem, and draw them.

- *Be the problem, or part of it*:
  Imagine that you are the troublesome part of the machine, or the lost or broken object, or the misunderstood message. Think hard about how you feel. What could be done? What would help?

- *Imagine something completely different*:
  Think of, imagine, anything – an object, an event, an idea; for instance, a spider's web, or a football match, or dissolving.
  Concentrate on this image in relation to the problem at hand. What's the link? Can you get a fresh perspective to help solve the problem?

- *Invert the problem*:
  Turn the problem inside out or upside down, or reverse it.
  For example, instead of putting a product into a package, consider putting a package round a product; instead of protecting employees from an industrial accident, protect the accident from the staff.

- *Turn the problem into an opportunity*:
  As the ancient saying has it, 'every problem is an opportunity'. For whom is this a problem? For whom is it an opportunity? Where is the opportunity in this?

■ *Write a story:*
Fictionalize the problem and the people concerned with it. How did it happen? Who does what next? How does it end? You could get a completely new angle on the situation.

Activity

Now choose one or more of the real problems from your work situation. Try each of the approaches on it:

■ Draw it.
■ Be the problem.
■ Imagine something completely different.
■ Invert the problem.
■ Think of the opportunities that could arise from the problem.
■ Write the story.

Note down all ideas and possible solutions – however fanciful.

In the light of the ideas you generate, reflect on which of the approaches helped you the most.

Follow-up

To become truly creative you must let yourself go a little. Try some of the other activities for developing creativity in this book and have a go.

The books listed under Activity 41, *Generating new ideas*, will also be useful here. Jane Henry's *Creative Management* (London: Sage/Open University, 2001) is a collection of good papers on all aspects of organization creativity. Edward de Bono is a prolific writer on this topic and you could try *Six Thinking Hats* (London: Penguin, 2000), *New Thinking for the New Millennium* (London: Penguin, 2000) or *Why So Stupid? How the Human Race has Never Really Learned to Think* (Black Rock, Co. Dublin: Blackhall Publishing, 2006).

Somewhat different is John Drysdale's *Discovery* (London: Cyan Books, 2005), which shows how valuable lessons and ideas can be found in unexpected places – including music, theatre, cinema, art and sport.

Attribute Alternatives

Learning areas	**Creativity**

We often get stuck in routine ways of doing things and locked in by our assumptions about the way things should be done.

A way to overcome these constraints is to identify the attributes of the current method and then generate a list of alternative attributes.

Activity

Step 1

Choose a current task that you suspect might be done differently or better. Note down the method or device currently in use, with its main characteristics and attributes.

For example, in the newspaper industry: take the threat to the conventional newspaper in the digital age. Current medium – broadsheet or tabloid conventional paper.

Step 2

Take each of the attributes and consider alternatives to it. You could use the approach in Activity 41, *Generating new ideas*, here.

List any alternatives that come to mind and do not attempt to evaluate them. No matter how silly or impractical it seems, list it. With the example above, the following alternatives are possible:

■ Made of: (paper) reprintable medium, reprogrammable special item, CD, downloadable.

■ Life: (disposable) returnable, refreshable, reprogrammable
■ Delivery: (shop or home delivery) phone, e-mail, 'cash point' style update of paper, mobile phone access etc.
■ Frequency: (daily/weekly) frequently, continuously, on access.

Step 3

Examine and evaluate the alternatives. Consider possible combinations. From the hundreds of potential permutations, choose some of the more likely combinations.

Examine these for practicability. Ideas might be logically or technically feasible, but have to be, and many people may still be uncomfortable with high-tech. delivery processes. We may value, e.g., conventional papers for other purposes – lighting fires, wrapping things, etc.

Follow-up

Keep trying out this exercise with real problems. Remember the important rule: generate as many alternatives as possible, but leave evaluation until later.

For further ideas you will find the sources listed under Activities 41, *Generating new ideas*, and 42, *Approaches to creativity*, of value.

Your Multiple Intelligences

Learning areas	**Mental agility:** Creativity: Self-knowledge

Howard Gardner's theory of multiple intelligences suggests that human beings possess many kinds of intelligence. He questions the idea of the single measure of general intelligence as simply measured by IQ tests:

"In the heyday of the psychometric and behaviorist eras, it was generally believed that intelligence was a single entity that was inherited; and that human beings – initially a blank slate – could be trained to learn anything, provided that it was presented in an appropriate way. Nowadays an increasing number of researchers believe precisely the opposite; that there exists a multitude of intelligences, quite independent of each other; that each intelligence has its own strengths and constraints; that the mind is far from unencumbered at birth; and that it is unexpectedly difficult to teach things that go against early 'naive' theories of that challenge the natural lines of force within an intelligence and its matching domains".

H. Gardner, 1993, xxiii

Although Gardner's theory has been criticized, it accords with much common-sense experience: we do think and learn in many different ways. There are eight types of intelligence in this theory:

- bodily/physical/kinaesthetic
- linguistic
- mathematical–logical
- visual/spatial
- musical
- interpersonal

- intrapersonal
- naturalist.

There are also various other possibilities being considered including spiritual, moral and existential intelligences.

Here is a questionnaire for you to assess your own multiple intelligences.

Activity

Step 1: Multiple intelligences questionnaire

Complete the questionnaire in Table A44.1 scoring 1–5 for each item depending upon how true this is of you.

Table A44.1 Multiple intelligences questionnaire

Item No.	Item	Score 1 – not true of me 2 – slightly true of me 3 – quite a bit true of me 4 – definitely true of me 5 – very true of me
1	I like to deal with problems physically, to get directly involved, get 'hands on'	
2	I appreciate books, radio, plays, poetry, playing with words	
3	I like to solve puzzles and problems	
4	I have a good sense of direction – where I am, which way I need to go	
5	I enjoy music – listening or playing	
6	I am interested in how other people think and feel	
7	I like to reflect on things that have happened and what I can learn from them	
8	I remember things about animals, birds, plants and so on	
9	I am skilful when working with things	
10	I learn well from books, lectures or tapes	
11	I like logical explanations	
12	I am observant, I notice what others do not	

13	I have a good sense of rhythm and/or melody	
14	I am sensitive to other peoples' moods and reactions	
15	I enjoy doing things independently of others	
16	I notice things in the environment that others often miss	
17	I enjoy physical activity – walking, dancing, games, swimming, etc.	
18	I talk well and have a large vocabulary	
19	I like to arrange tasks in a neat and orderly sequences	
20	I can see things clearly in 'my mind's eye' (e.g. a familiar room)	
21	I find it easy to learn songs and lyrics	
22	I can help with difficulties between people	
23	I appreciate privacy and quiet for working and thinking	
24	I am concerned about the environment and of endangered species	
25	I like to be moving, doing and touching things that I am learning about	
26	I am good at explaining things	
27	I look for patterns and relationships between things	
28	I find that films, slides, videos, pictures help me to learn	
29	I enjoy listening to sounds in nature	
30	I get involved in clubs, groups and social activities	
31	I reflect on my own feelings and thoughts and why I do things	
32	My sensory skills of sight, sound, taste, smell, touch are keen	
33	I remember best what I have done – compared with what I have seen or heard	
34	I like to write things down, take notes	
35	I approach tasks/problems in a logical, step-by-step way	
36	I like to use charts, diagrams, mind maps, pictures to help me to learn	

(Continued)

Table A44.1   (*Continued*)

Item No.	Item	Score 1 – not true of me 2 – slightly true of me 3 – quite a bit true of me 4 – definitely true of me 5 – very true of me
37	I can easily remember tunes	
38	I enjoy discussing things and ideas with others	
39	I like to think about the purpose of what I am doing and learning	
40	I easily learn characteristics, names, categorization and data about objects or species found in the natural world	

Step 2: Scoring

Now score the questionnaire in Table A44.2, adding up the numbers for each of the items listed against each of the multiple intelligence categories.

The maximum score is 25 and the minimum is 5.

Table A44.2   Multiple intelligences scoring key

'Intelligence'	Item numbers	Total score
Bodily/physical/kinaesthetic	1, 9, 17, 25, 33	
Linguistic	2, 10, 18, 26, 34	
Mathematical–logical	3, 11, 19, 27, 35	
Visual/spatial	4, 12, 20, 28, 36	
Musical	5, 13, 21, 29, 37	
Interpersonal	6, 14, 22, 30, 38	
Intrapersonal	7, 15, 23, 31, 39	
Naturalist	8, 16, 24, 32, 40	

Step 3: So what?

Now map your eight intelligence scores on to the 'spider's web' in Fig. A44.1.

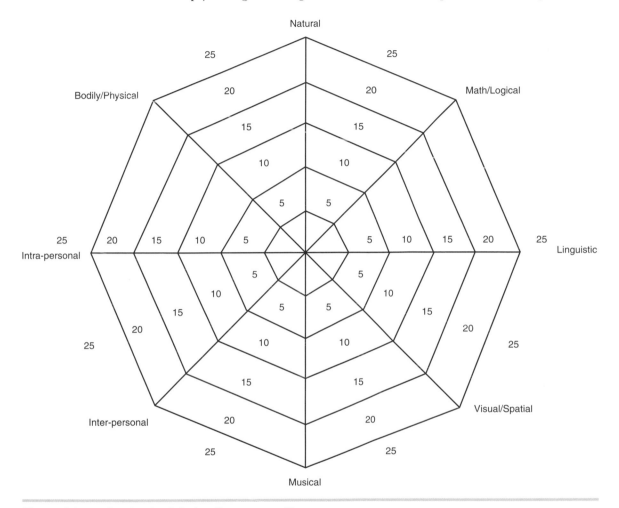

Figure A44.1   Gardner's eight intelligences profile

The 'spider's web' enables you to draw up a profile of your scores on each of the eight intelligences. What does your profile mean? Here are a few possibilities to get you thinking:

▬ If you scored between 20 and 25 in any one dimension then you are high in this form of intelligence; if you scored from 5 to 10, then this is an underdeveloped area for you.

- The profile can indicate your current preferences, and also those areas of experience that you currently avoid. One way to work with this is deliberately to try to use your less favoured intelligences; for example, if you are high on intrapersonal, but low on interpersonal, then make yourself go and talk with other people about issues that you would normally keep to yourself.
- Conversely, if you are very high on interpersonal, but low on intrapersonal, then take time out alone to reflect on what something might be telling you, what it means for you. How do you personally think and feel about it?
- If you are low on spatial intelligence, draw a picture of a situation that you find yourself in at work or at home.
- Another possibility is that you might find that you are high on an intelligence that you don't get an opportunity to use at work. In this case, what sort of work would enable you to exploit your talent? Who, in your organization, uses this sort of ability? Go and talk to them, exploring how you could do more with what you've got.

These are only a few of the possibilities arising from assessing your multiple intelligences. To take this further, you probably need to read more about the idea and consult with other people about what this might mean for you.

Follow-up

Howard Gardner's classic text is *Frames of Mind: The Theory of Multiple Intelligences* (New York: Basic Books, 1993). A more recent book is a useful review of the theory and a discussion of issues, additions and criticisms: *Intelligence Reframed. Multiple Intelligences for the 21st Century* (New York: Basic Books, 1999).

As ever, there is a great deal on the web. Enter 'multiple intelligences' and this will bring you more than you can deal with. You could start with *infed*, which is an independent not-for-profit site put together by a small group of educators: www.infed.org/thinkers/gardner.htm.

Activity 45

Coping with Complexity

Learning areas	**Mental agility:** Emotional resilience

Too much change in too short a time can result in stress and disorientation in rats and humans.

Coping with and adapting to change call for great effort in terms of emotional stability and of learning new skills and new knowledge.

Mental agility or 'flexible intelligence' is an ability – potential or realized – which all of us have to some extent. Unlike this old-fashioned and fixed view of 'intelligence' as associated with crude tests of 'general intelligence' or 'IQ', mental agility can be improved with practice like any other skill.

Mental agility is the ability which allows us to do several things at once, switching our minds and resources from one topic to another, making hundreds of decisions as we do so, storing information, recalling it – in short, what we all do in a multi-task situations.

Consider the mental agility requirements of the parent's job, e.g.:

Prepare breakfast for four people *simultaneously with*:

- finding and putting together two lots of dinner money
- cleaning two pairs of shoes
- listening to the news on the radio
- brushing two lots of hair
- talking lovingly to partner
- talking lovingly to children
- dealing with sundry contingencies – all in 30 minutes.

How did you get on?

There are many forms of complex work, which we learn and then do instinctively. The teacher in a classroom, the retail supervisor, the team manager, all pursue multiple tasks, observe thousands of stimuli, attend to a few, make appropriate multiple responses and so on. And all without much conscious thought about the complexity of the situation. We don't usually reflect on our complex skills and how this learning may be applied as a general skill to new situations.

Activity

This activity invites you to work on certain multiple tasks and consciously reflect about how you are adapting to the skill requirements of doing several simultaneous tasks.

Step 1

Find a free hour for this activity (a tough task in itself). Now choose six tasks, suitable for your particular circumstances, e.g. if you are at work, these could include:

- writing a paper or notes for a meeting
- planning your key outputs for the next six months
- catching up with your e-mails
- telephoning three or four people you need to contact
- talking to a colleague about something which interests them
- preparing statistics
- filling in government forms (an Inland Revenue form is ideal)
- planning the best new arrangement for your workspace
- reading a management book
- doing *The Times* crossword.

Step 2

Estimate how long each task will take; add up the total time and halve it (you only ever have half the time you need).

Now, try to complete all the tasks in that time. Don't do them sequentially, do them all at once, switching from one to another.

NB: If you find switching from one task to another hard, then do it mechanically. Number the tasks 1 to 6; divide your allotted time and, using a dice, change tasks after every 3 or 5 minutes. This will be difficult at first, but your flexibility will improve.

Step 3

Now reflect on your experience. Note down your responses to the following questions:

1. *How did I do in terms of completing the tasks?*

_____

_____

_____

2. *What feelings did I have during this experiment?* (Record all the phrases/ adjectives that spring to mind.)

_____

_____

_____

3. *Have I ever felt like this before? When? What was the outcome then?*

_____

_____

_____

4. *Could I have been better organized or better prepared? How would I do it better next time?*

_____

_____

_____

5. *How can I increase my general ability to deal with multi-task situations?*

_____

_____

_____

To exercise and increase your mental agility, repeat this experiment in other situations. The important thing is to be aware of what you are doing and when you are doing it.

Always make time for reflection afterwards. Without this you may miss the learning potential of your own experiences.

Follow-up

Complexity is a topic in itself. For a simple introduction to Complexity Theory you could look at Sardar and Abrams' *Introducing Chaos* (Thriplow: Icon Books, 1999, 2003). Biologist Roger Lewin's book *Complexity* (London: Phoenix, 1993) critically examines the ideas of complexity.

Ralph Stacey applies these ideas to management and organizations in *Complexity and Creativity in Organisations* (San Francisco: Berrett Koehler, 1996). Since then, the same author has written a number of related books, including, with Douglas Griffin and Patricia Shaw, *Complexity and Management: Fad or Radical Challenge to Systems Thinking?* (London: Routledge, 2000); *Complexity and Group Processes: A Radically Social Understanding of Individuals* (London: Brunner-Routledge, 2003); and, as Editor with Douglas Griffin, *Complexity and the Experience of Leading Organisations* (London: Routledge, 2005).

Just a Minute

The nature of leadership and managerial work demands the ability to think through complex matters, to think quickly on one's feet and to switch rapidly from one problem to another.

There is a widely held belief that intelligence is innate and cannot be developed through training. This idea comes from early psychological theories which have long since been questioned and rejected. Current thinking suggests that the kind of mental abilities that make up intelligence can improve significantly through experience and practice. The following activity is designed to give you practice in thinking quickly on your feet.

Activity

You need ten filing cards or small pieces of paper, and a tape recorder.

Step 1

Write one of the following topics on each of five cards:

- home working
- self-managed team working
- e-commerce
- workaholism
- safety.

Step 2

On each of the remaining five cards, write one of the following audiences:

- group of government inspectors
- party of visiting Korean business people
- visiting party of final-year university undergraduates
- party of South American tourists
- group of senior citizens.

Shuffle the two sets of cards separately and put the two piles face down.

Step 3

Turn on the tape recorder. Pick up the first card on each pile and talk for one minute on the revealed topic, to the indicated audience. After a minute, pick up the second topic and audience cards and talk for another minute. Repeat this until you have used all the cards.

Play back the tape to review how well you did in keeping to the topic and relating it to the audience in each instance.

Obviously, if you wish, choose your own topics and audiences to suit your situation better.

Follow-up

Thinking skills come with practice, so the more you can exercise them, the more they will develop.

You should be able to find plenty of opportunities for this in the context of your work. If you want to test yourself on IQ-type tests, there are many of these on the web. Management and business bookshops also sell practice versions of the Princeton Test – the one most often used for selection to Business School MBA programmes.

Activity 47

A Helicopter Mind

An extensive study of managers concluded that the 'helicopter mind' quality is a key determinant of success. This is the ability to think in both concrete and abstract terms, and to move rapidly between the two, linking abstract ideas to specific actions and vice versa. Leaders and managers who think in this way are good at linking theory to practice so that each improves the other.

Whether thinking moves 'up' to the abstract or 'down' to the specific depends on the questions asked: 'Why?' questions move you up, 'How?' questions move you down.

For example, the task of selecting people can be analysed in this way:

WHY? – To produce enough to meet orders

↑

WHY? – To get good enough people to work the machines

↑

TASK – SELECT PEOPLE FOR JOBS

↓

HOW? – Assess skills needed, test applicants for these

↓

HOW? – Study existing staff, develop tests to demonstrate skills

If you start with a statement of fact, you can ask: WHY is this true? And HOW can this be applied? For example, see Fig. A47.1.

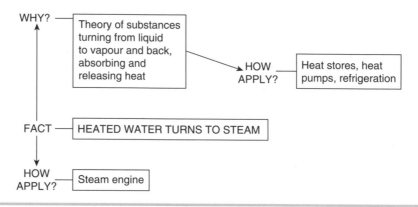

Figure A47.1 *'How' and 'why' thinking*

Once the 'Why?' questions are answered, moving down again with 'How?' questions can help generate new alternatives and ideas. In the example above, the answer to the 'Why?' question can become the new task from which to generate more 'How?' ideas (as illustrated in Fig. A47.2):

TASK – To produce enough to meet orders

HOW? – Get more people to work machines *or* get faster machines

HOW? – Offer overtime *or* recruit more people

The Activity below offers you an opportunity to practise using both 'How?' and 'Why?' questions to analyse *activities* and *facts* relevant to your work.

Activity

Choose a current and problematic task or 'fact' connected to your work.

Write the task, activity or fact in the middle of a sheet of flipchart of paper and build your answers to the 'How?' and 'Why?' questions around it. It will look something like Fig. A47.2.

In doing this activity, and in your thinking in general, you should aim to ask both 'How?' and 'Why?' questions and not just one or the other. This is the way to develop a helicopter mind, so that you can both hover above the problem *and* get right down to the details (or vice versa), and repeat this as often as you need to understand the situation truly.

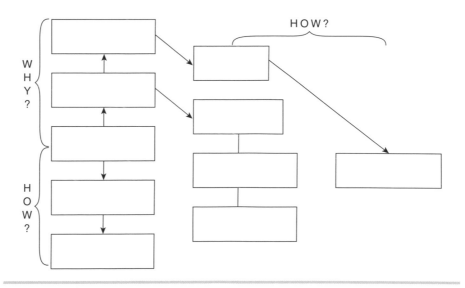

Figure 47.2   *'How' and 'why' activity*

Follow-up

You may find it useful to use some of your 'How'/'Why' analyses as the basis for discussion with others who share the same concerns.

If you are interested in IQ, then *The IQ and Psychometric Test Workbook*, by Philip Carter (London: Kogan Page, 2005) is a self-test book. If you want to go further and improve your IQ rather than just measure it, then you might enjoy Philip Carter and Ken Russell's *Increase Your Brainpower: Improve Your Creativity, Memory, Mental Agility and Intelligence* (Chichester: Wiley, 2001). And if you really like that sort of thing, then the website for the 'intelligence' club, MENSA, is www.mensa.org.uk/mensa/global/resource.html.

On the other hand, the whole concept of IQ is increasingly challenged as rather narrow. Tony Buzan's *Head First* (London: HarperCollins, 2000) suggests thinking about your many forms of intelligence (see also Activity 44, *Your multiple intelligences*, and the sources listed here) will be useful.

Daniel Goleman's influential *Emotional Intelligence* (anniversary 10th edition, New York: Bantam, 2005) is amplified in a number of related books such as *The Emotional Intelligence Quick Book: Everything You Need to Know to Put Your EQ to Work*, by Travis Bradberry and Jean Graves (New York: Fireside/Simon and Schuster, 2005).

Managing Your Dependency

Learning areas	**Balanced learning habits**

The theme of this book is *self-development*, which holds that for real learning to occur you need to take personal responsibility for your own learning.

This means moving from:

- *Dependence* – or accepting uncritically any instructions from teachers and other people with formal authority as the 'right way' to do things, to:
- *Independence* – or taking and ideas from teachers and authority figures as suggestions which you may try out and evaluate for yourself, adding them to your repertoire of skills and practices if *you* judge them to work.

The *independence* philosophy can be overdone and lead to an obstinate unwillingness to accept any guidance from qualified people.

- *Interdependence* – or *mature dependency* means making full use of the advice from people with genuine expertise and experience. In this way, wisdom is passed from person to person and generation to generation, so that we can benefit from others' past successes and failures and, in turn, pass on what we consider to be useful knowledge.

Activity

Step 1

Make a list of six or so major tasks or activities which you have to perform in your work: preparing budgets, negotiating and bargaining, designing new products or procedures, providing leadership for a team or group, advising others, selling things or ideas, planning operations, interviewing and so on. Write them down in the first column of Table A48.1.

Table A48.1

Task/activity	Are you an expert?	Do you know of an expert?	Do you believe an expert exists?	Or is it an, as yet, unsolved problem?

Step 2

Take each of these in turn, go through the questions below, stopping at the first one that you can answer 'yes' to. Put a tick in the appropriate column of Table A48.1 for each task or activity depending upon which of questions a, b, c or d you first answer 'yes' to. There should be only one tick in the table for each task or activity.

(a) In terms of the practical ability to carry out this task or activity, do you see yourself as expert, and that you can reliably deal with it?

(b) If no to a, is there an expert or source of expertise that you know of who could provide you with help on this task?

(c) If no to a and b, do you believe that somewhere an expert exists – a procedure, approach or person who can provide a reliable solution to carrying out the task?

(d) If no to a, b and c, is this then one of those tasks or problems for which no known solution exists at this time, and therefore that you have as good a chance as anyone else of finding one?

Step 3

Now treat each of your answers as a statement to be *tested*. Consider what *evidence* you have. Are you really fully competent? Can the 'expert' really produce results? Can you track down an expert or authoritative source of knowledge on the problem?

■ Consider whether your personality leads you to believe in, seek out and rely on experts, or whether you tend to go it alone. Does this help or hinder you?

It will be particularly useful if you show your conclusions to someone else who is familiar with the same tasks and problems, and who will give you an honest opinion about your conclusions.

■ Does your organization have a culture of relying on experts or of finding its own solutions? Does this work well or not?

Follow-up

You may find it useful to follow up this activity by exploring what expertise exists to deal with problems facing you. Try sources on the web, within your own organization, in libraries or in educational institutions in your area.

John Burgoyne's *Developing Yourself, Your Career and Your Organisation*. (London: Lemos and Crane, 1999) provides a guide to taking over managing your development in the context of work.

Learning to Learn

Learning areas	**Balanced learning habits:** Self-knowledge: Sensitivity to events

There are five stages to learning a new skill or ability:

- Becoming aware of inadequacies in the way you do things and sensing a need for new behaviour.
- Identifying the behaviours involved in a new skill or activity.
- Practising these behaviours.
- Seeking and getting feedback on your performance.
- Integrating the behaviours into your repertoire of skills and abilities.

Lifelong learning is especially vital for managers and leaders because of their challenging and changing responsibilities. We used to believe that most human learning was done in the first five years of life; but more recently, we have become aware of the need and potential for continuing learning throughout life. Being able to learn from everyday experience is a skill in itself.

Learning to learn is therefore a new and vital activity for managers and leaders. This activity helps you to reflect on how you acquired your existing repertoire of skills and abilities, and also with thinking about what you need to learn next and in the future.

Activity

Step 1

Think of two incidents in the past year where you have been successful – 'high spots' or 'peak experiences' – the sort of thing you would talk about in a promotion interview to demonstrate your strengths.

Now describe these events – what actually happened and what did you do exactly? Write these down and be as *specific* as you can.

Event 1

What happened?

_____

_____

_____

What did you do?

_____

_____

_____

Event 2

What happened?

_____

_____

_____

What did you do?

_____

_____

_____

Step 2

From these two events, what were the key *skills* and *qualities* that enabled you to do what you did and to achieve a successful outcome?

Table A49.1   Learning skills

Skill/ability	Where did I learn it from?	How did I learn it?
1.		
2.		
3.		
4.		
5.		
6.		

Write these down in column 1 of Table A49.1. Then answer these two questions for each key skill or quality:

(a) *Where* did I learn it from?
  - the boss?
  - school/college?
  - from doing the job?
  - a book?
  - from my colleagues? etc.

It is also useful to recall over what period of time and at what stage in your life this skill/ability was learned. Do this by remembering the latest time when you are sure you *did not* have the skill or ability and the earliest time you *did*.

(b) How did I learn it, i.e. what process was involved? For example, by:
  - being told something?
  - imitating somebody?
  - puzzling it out for myself?
  - accident or on purpose?
  - through emotional or intellectual channels?
  - etc.

Step 3

From the data generated in Steps 1 and 2, write down the insights you have had so far about *how* you learn.

When you have noted as much as you can, reflect on the following questions about your learning processes. Write down any additional insights you get from answering these questions:

(a) Do the five stages of learning a new skill or ability fit with your learning experiences or not?

_____

_____

_____

(b) Do you learn different things in different ways? If so, what things and in what ways?

_____

_____

_____

(c) Thinking about other people that you know well, are there any learning processes that they use which you do not?

_____

_____

_____

(d) Do you learn from receiving 'inputs' – being told or shown something?

_____

_____

_____

(e) Do you learn from imitating other people or by observing the success and failures of their actions?

_____

_____

_____

(f) What is the place of emotion and feelings in your learning? Is learning painful, pleasant or what for you?

_____

_____

_____

Step 4

Find a friend, colleague or perhaps a trainer or facilitator and discuss your reflections with them. Working with other people in this way – sharing, listening, questioning, reflecting together – is a key learning process in adults and one you need to employ frequently if you are to become the lifelong learner *and* the manager and leader that you can truly be.

Follow-up

Learning how to learn is not easy and is, perhaps, the ultimate leadership and management skill. Understanding your learning processes is one way to improve your ability to learn. Work on this, and the rest of the managerial skills and abilities come much more easily.

New approaches to learning include the use of Gardner's eight intelligences (see Activity 44) and a related field that has become known as 'Accelerated Learning'. Most books on this are written for teachers rather than learners. Exceptions are Ricki Linksman's *How to Learn Anything Quickly: An Accelerated Program for Rapid Learning* (Replica Books, 1999) and Colin Rose's *Accelerated Learning for the 21st Century: The Six-Step Plan to Unlock Your Master-mind* (New York: Dell, 1998). You might also be willing to try Lynda Hudson's *Revise and Remember (Older Children, Students and Adults): Study Aid – Latest Accelerated Learning Techniques*, (Firstwayforward CDs, 2004), which is described as 'a self-help hypnotherapy CD'.

A different approach, using seven modes of learning, is Tom Boydell's *Doing Things Well, Doing Things Better, Doing Better Things: A Guide to Effective Learning* (Sheffield: Inter-Logics, 2001), available electronically at *tboydell@inter-logics.net*.

Everybody learns more and more easily in a Learning Company. Mike Pedler, Tom Boydell and John Burgoyne's *The Learning Company: A Strategy for Sustainable Development* (2nd edition, Maidenhead: McGraw-Hill, 1996) contains ideas and 101 'Glimpses' on what a Learning Company is. Peter Senge and colleagues' *The Fifth Discipline Fieldbook. Strategies and Tools for Building a Learning Organisation* (New York: Doubleday Currency and London: Nicholas Brealey, 1994) is full of interesting material on learning disciplines, disabilities and systems thinking.

Study Skills

Learning areas	**Balanced learning habits:** Professional knowledge: Self-knowledge

We sometimes say 'she or he is very clever' of someone who is highly qualified, implying that they are more able than the rest of us. Professional qualifications are often taken as a measure of a person's worth, and people of ability are handicapped by the lack of them. But basic ability is only one part of obtaining professional qualifications; opportunity and chance are often of equal significance.

Another critical aspect is application – sticking to the task – and this includes skills in studying. Study skills are different from some other components of academic success because you are not born with them and you do not acquire them by chance. You have to learn them.

Study skills are important whether you are professionally qualified or not. They are important to all leaders and managers because they contribute to that illusive skill of being able to learn from one's own experience (see Activity 49, *Learning to learn*).

Start by looking at your own study skills. There is insufficient space here to become proficient in all these skills, but this activity will help you make a diagnosis and provide pointers for your next steps.

Activity

Step 1: Questionnaire 1 – study tasks

The *very best* way to use this questionnaire is to complete it *prior* to some period of study, and then after to see if you feel you have made an improvement.

To get an estimate of your existing level of study skills, complete Questionnaire 1 (Table A50.1) by circling 3, 2 or 1 for each of the 16 questions.

Table A50.1   Questionnaire 1 – study tasks

	This is a big problem for me	This is something of a problem for me	This is not a problem for me
For each question, circle one number – 1, 2 or 3 – in the columns at the right			
Here are some tasks which have to be achieved for successful study			
'How difficult is it for you to …			
1. … decide on a suitable *place* for studying?	3	2	1
2. … decide *when* to study, or for *how long*?	3	2	1
3. … choose your goal (i.e. precisely what you want to learn)?	3	2	1
4. … decide *how* to achieve your goal (i.e. what study activities to perform)?	3	2	1
5. … obtain or reach people, books and other *resources*?	3	2	1
6. … deal with *lack of desire* for achieving your goal, once set?	3	2	1
7. … deal with *dislike of activities* necessary to reach your goal (e.g. you want to learn Spanish but you hate reading)?	3	2	1
8. … cope with *doubts* about success	3	2	1
9. … *estimate level of knowledge or skill* – start and finish and also during study to determine progress?	3	2	1
10. … deal with *difficulty in understanding* some part or through lack of fundamental knowledge at some stage?	3	2	1
11. … be able to *concentrate*?	3	2	1
12. … be able to *remember*?	3	2	1
13. … be able to *apply* knowledge gained to real-life situations?	3	2	1
14. … deal with *frustration* arising from speed to learning, material containing opinions rather than clear-cut 'facts'?	3	2	1
15. … be able to overcome laziness or inertia despite interest?	3	2	1
16. … find fellow learners for mutual stimulation and companionship?'	3	2	1

Scoring

Add up the circled numbers.

The measurement that matters is one which matches you against yourself and not against some mythical standard. However …

■ If you scored less than 20, you have few study problems (at least as revealed by this questionnaire).

■ If you scored between 20 and 30, you do have some difficulties. You need to do more work on your study skills.

■ If you scored over 30, it is highly likely that your innate ability is being held back by inadequate study skills.

Step 2

Remembering that this questionnaire is only as valid as *you* think it is, go back through it and look at the questions where you circled 3. Then study the ones where you circled 2. Where are the difficulties?

For example, an inability to concentrate or to maintain motivation (both very common study problems) may be caused by a huge variety of things. There may be a very simple reason, such as working in a noisy or unsuitable environment; or it may be exceedingly complex. Lack of concentration is a frequent result of emotional upset, and lack of motivation may stem from a deep-seated fear of failure, perhaps developed in childhood.

There are a wide variety of possible interpretations of your results. You might find it helpful to think through your results with a supportive person who can help you reflect.

Step 3: Solutions

Whatever your study difficulties, the good news is that there are answers, things that you can do to improve your skills. Depending on where the difficulties are located, here are some possible ways forward:

■ Set yourself a STUDY DIARY, giving specific periods on given days of the week for study (Questions 2; 6; 7; 11; 15).

■ Find a good PLACE for you to study (this may be combined with time) (Questions 1; 2; 5; 15; 16).

■ Establish a SELF-TESTING procedure (Questions 6; 8; 9).

■ Establish a rigorous PRACTICE ROUTINE (Questions 6; 7; 11; 12).

■ Join a suitable study CLASS (Questions 4; 5; 9; 10; 15; 16).

■ Consult an EXPERT or TUTOR (Questions 4; 5; 9; 10).

■ Set yourself a detailed ACTION PLAN (Questions 3; 4; 5; 9).

And *especially*:

■ Find a supportive FRIEND or ALLY – to talk, to swap ideas, to counsel, to encourage, to discipline, etc. (all questions).

These are only some of the possible solutions (see Follow-up).

Step 4: Questionnaire 2 – study skills

So far we have been considering overall study tasks – the problems to be overcome when studying usually alone and without a tutor; but there are also specific skills involved in studying, such as reading, writing, etc.

Now complete Questionnaire 2 (Table A50.2).

Table A50.2   Questionnaire 2 – study skills

	Rarely	Sometimes	Usually
For each question, circle one number – 1, 2 or 3 – in the columns at the right			
Here are some tasks which have to be achieved for successful study			
'Do you …			
1. … decide in advance *what* you are going to study and *where*?	1	2	3
2. … set yourself goals and subgoals (e.g. I will read this book between now and then; 30 pages here, etc.)?	1	2	3
3. … meet your deadlines – especially with regard to written work, reports, etc.?	1	2	3
4. … read fast enough to read all the books you need to read on any given matter?	1	2	3
5. … skim or scan through books using contents pages and indexes, before deciding what to read?	1	2	3
6. … consciously read for a purpose (i.e. to gain specific material and not just to 'get everything')?	1	2	3
7. … find it possible to concentrate when listening to lectures or talks?	1	2	3
8. … take notes when listening to talks or lectures?	1	2	3
9. … know how to use library systems to find the books or information you need?	1	2	3
10. … write key notes (i.e. headings and sub-headings rather than continuous prose)?	1	2	3
11. … feel at ease drawing up reports or writing papers?	1	2	3
12. … express yourself well in writing?'	1	2	3

Scoring

Questionnaire 2 focuses on several key areas of study skill:

- organizing yourself and your time
- reading
- listening to talks or lectures
- note taking
- writing.

You should aim to be consistently circling 3s in this questionnaire.

Good study skills and habits take time and purposeful practice to master. You need to keep practising over time and with persistence until you have developed these useful habits. Good luck.

Follow-up

There are many, many books and resources on study skills. Search the web or consult your local training department, library or college and they will be certain to have something to offer.

Some of the references in the previous Activity will also be relevant here. In addition, Oliver Caviglioli and Ian Harris's *Mapwise: Accelerated Learning Through Visible Thinking* (Stafford: Network Educational Press, 2000) is an excellent description of how to use mapping to look at note taking, memorizing and developing ideas.

The Good Study Guide, by Andrew Northedge (Maidenhead: Open University/McGraw-Hill, 2005) covers ways of studying, essay writing and preparing for examinations.

Your Learning Cycle

Your learning cycle is founded upon the key learning experiences in your life. This Activity, taken together the previous Activities 49, *Learning to learn,* and 50, *Study skills*, will increase your learning abilities, which is a major goal of this book.

In adults, learning happens when we become dissatisfied with our behaviour in the light of various experiences. If we are open and willing to learn, reflecting on our experiences can give us clues to new and more satisfying actions.

On the other hand, adults have so much accumulated experience that often this past experience gets in the way of the new: "I have 10 years' experience of interviewing, I think I know most of what there is to know!"

Unexamined life events are not experiences – just things that happened. Experience is generated when we reflect. And this reflection can lead, often in small ways, to changed perceptions of situations and new ways in which we might act. This process or learning cycle looks like Fig. A51.1.

Activity

Each of us is a unique blend of inherited characteristics modified over time by all sorts of experiences – some pleasant, some less so. And it is often these painful experiences that teach us the most.

In this activity you are invited to re-live some of these past experiences. What made them so important in making you the person you are today?

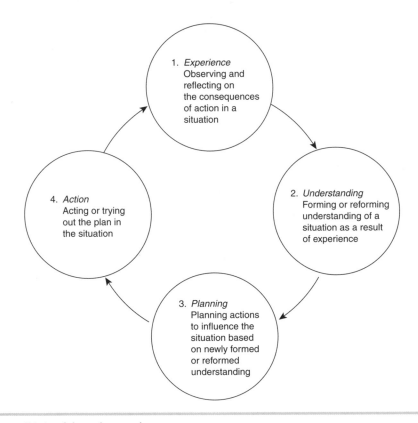

Figure 51.1   A learning cycle

Step 1

Think of the key learning experiences in your life – those that led to significant change in your long-term actions and behaviour.

Pick three, four or five of these key learning experiences. They may have been short or long in duration, but they must have resulted in a discernible changes in the way you behaved. Give each a title or phrase to label it. Here are some examples:

- being punished
- going to school for the first time
- first love affair
- having a baby
- becoming able to work a personal computer
- broken leg
- university degree
- being praised.

Step 2

Take a piece of paper for each experience and label it. Divide the sheet into eight parts with horizontal lines and makes some notes in response to the following questions:

1. *What happened?*

_____

_____

_____

2. *What started it?*

_____

_____

_____

3. *What did you learn?*

_____

_____

_____

4. *What words describe how you felt while it was happening?*

_____

_____

_____

5. *Who else was involved?*

_____

_____

_____

6. *Did they help or hinder your learning? How?*

_____

_____

_____

7. *How would you describe the learning process?*

_____

_____

_____

8. *What were the key characteristics of this event – as compared with others in your life when you didn't learn as much?*

_____

_____

_____

Step 3

When you have completed sheets for three, four or five key learning experiences, look back through them and seek out and connections and commonalities that you can see – in how things started; in how you felt; in who was involved, etc. Can you see any patterns in your learning experiences?

Note these down.

_____

_____

_____

_____

_____

Now look back through your learning experiences and make two lists: what factors *helped* you to learn, and what *hindered* your learning?:

Factors assisting learning	Factors hindering learning
(i)	(i)
(ii)	(ii)
(iii)	(iii)
(iv)	(iv)
(v)	(v)
(vi)	(vi)
etc.	etc.

Your key learning experiences are the source of the skills and abilities that you possess today. Understanding your learning cycle and patterns will help you get the best lessons from your future experiences as a manager and leader.

Follow-up

This activity is closely linked with the previous Activities 49, *Learning to learn*, and 50, *Study skills*. The books listed there are also relevant here.

The learning cycle is found in David Kolb's *Experiential Learning* (London: Prentice-Hall, 1985), which is a good book on how adults learn. Building on this, Peter Honey and Alan Mumford's *Using Your Learning Styles* (Maidenhead: Peter Honey Publications, 1986) and Alan Mumford's *Effective Learning* (London: CIPD, 1999) offer analyses of your learning style and useful ways of thinking about better learning.

Conversations with Yourself

Learning areas	**Self-knowledge:** Creativity

Talking to yourself – according to the playground joke – is a sign of madness. In art history, 'madness' and creativity are often closely linked and that what was once described as lunacy would now be called non-conformity or even genius. It is often the abnormality in famous people, a deviation from some norm, that makes them outstanding. This is linked to psychologists' concepts such as divergent and convergent thinking or vertical and lateral thinking. It seems that a certain amount of experimentation and playfulness is necessary for creativity and learning.

This activity is simple, straightforward and powerful. You'll need a tape recorder, a private room and some uninterrupted time.

Activity

Step 1

Go into your room, lock the door, switch on the tape recorder and begin speaking to *yourself*. Do not address any audience or person, real or imaginary. Speak to yourself.

You may find this quite difficult or it may be quite natural to you. If you find it hard, you may need several starts before you get into it.

If you have any doubts, play back what you've said and check whether you are *really speaking to yourself*.

Step 2

When you have mastered talking to yourself, start on any specific problem or difficult situation facing you. Keep talking until you have said everything you wish to say about this situation.

Step 3

Play back the tape. Listen until you are satisfied that you understand yourself.

Step 4

Wipe off the tape before leaving the room – whether you achieved Steps 2 and 3 in their entirety or not. *This is extremely important.*

Step 5

Repeat Steps 1–4 periodically as a means of getting in touch with the problem.

This activity is a formal way of thinking aloud – a more respectable occupation than talking to yourself. The theory is that whenever we speak, we speak to an audience. We always try to impress or achieve a specific effect upon another or others. We rarely, if ever, speak to ourselves to find out *what we really think.*

Creativity seems to be only partly a conscious process. There is only so much that can be done by the conscious mind. Often the 'aha!' or 'eureka!' experience comes after we have slept on or dropped a problem to think about something else. The assumption is that the unconscious mind worked somehow on the original situation and emerged with a solution or breakthrough.

Try it – you may break that block you've been struggling with for so long.

Follow-up

The books suggested in Activities 41, *Generating new ideas*, and 42, *Approaches to creativity*, offer ways forward in developing your thinking and creativity.

Backwards Review

Learning areas	**Self-knowledge:** Sensitivity to events

The ancient dictum 'know thyself' is as applicable to today's leaders and managers as it was to the sages who coined it. To know myself – how I act and behave; what my strengths, weaknesses and learning needs are; what motivates and excites me; what scares and dismays me; the effects I have on others; and the effects different people have on me are all important aspects of managing myself and leading others.

When we're going out, or off to an important meeting, we may check out how we look – by glancing in the mirror. Knowing ourselves requires this sort of information, this reflection from some mirror. *Backwards review* is a reflective meditation which creates the mirror for ourselves. It is very simple and also quite profound. It takes practice to develop.

Activity

Step 1

This is a simple yet profound activity for becoming more aware of yourself and your situation. You can do it at any time, but it works well after any significant episode: after an argument, an important meeting, a momentous event, at the end of a year. It takes practice to develop this skill, but it is a fundamental way of developing awareness and consciousness.

It is perhaps best done at the end of each day, just before you go to sleep.

Step 2

Find a quiet place to be and do the activity. You can do it sitting up, lying down, walking – whatever, as long it is a place for yourself free from interruption and distraction.

Step 3

Now begin to go through the events of the day (or meeting, week, month, etc.) in your mind:

Work *backwards*, starting with the most recent happenings.

■ Try to recall what happened in each event or episode – what did you do? What were you thinking at the time? What feelings were you having?
■ What did you actually want to do at that time and what did you actually do?
■ What were other people doing and what were their thoughts, feelings and wishes?

(As you can see by now, this 'simple' exercise is quite a challenge. Do not give up.)

■ Try to picture, to visualize, what happened. Take each episode in turn going slowly backwards, bringing the picture of it into your mind.

(Some people find it easy to see pictures in their minds, others find it very hard.)

■ What did you do? What were others doing?
■ How did you feel? What were your thoughts? … and so on.

Step 4

Keep going as slowly as you like until you get to the end (actually the beginning) of the day (or meeting, week, etc.).

Don't be discouraged if you don't get this far and can only manage a few episodes or hours back. You could start just with an hour or so, and gradually extend the time.

If you work to develop this skill, you will become much more conscious of yourself, your actions, your thoughts and your feelings. You will also gain insights into those of other people, and see more clearly what effects them and how their actions, thoughts and feelings affect you.

This reflective skill is one that you can use whenever you need it, especially perhaps when your mind feels dull or you need to be extra vigilant.

Follow-up

You follow this Activity by taking lots of practice. If you like it and want to explore further the processes of managing yourself, try Mike Pedler and Tom Boydell's *Managing Yourself* (London: Lemos and Crane, 1999).